Contents

KW-484-864

introduction

Political Philosophy in concerned with the basic principles and values that underpin political life. It asks 'What is the best way of organizing society in order to allow all its citizens to enjoy the good life?' It sets about trying to balance the desire for freedom against the need for justice, and the right of an individual to better himself or herself against a need for fairness and protection for the poorest in society.

While the study of Politics looks at the way in which political institutions *are* organized, Political Philosophy stands back and examines the principles by which they *should* be organized. As such, it is absolutely fundamental to an appreciation of political argument.

In this chapter we shall examine briefly what Political Philosophy sets out to do, and then take an historical overview of political ideas and issues from ancient Greece to the present day, setting the agenda for what is to follow.

Political philosophy is about good government – what it involves, how it is regulated and how it is brought about. It is about the principles that help us to decide whether or not any particular government is to be judged good or bad. And, of course, that requires an examination of the fundamental principles of government – why we need it, what its goals should be, how it is to be regulated and how, if it goes wrong, it may be repaired or replaced.

Political philosophy may be seen as a branch of ethics, or moral philosophy. Ethics looks at all issues of right and wrong in the way people treat one another, while political philosophy limits itself to the specific issues related to our collective or political life. It is the ethics of social organization, applied across society, rather than between individuals. So, for example, utilitarianism as an ethical theory (seeking that which appears to offer the greatest benefit for the greatest number) when applied to society as a whole, is used to justify democracy, which aims to take the preferences of all citizens into account through the democratic process.

But just as ethics requires us to give a rational justification for our actions, so too political philosophy examines the justification for political institutions and ideologies. Is democracy fair to everyone? Is there such a thing as a good dictatorship? It also examines key ideas – fairness, justice, the rights of individuals or communities – to see how they are related to one another, and how what they describe may be achieved.

Would it be fair if everyone in society received an equal share of goods and services, no matter what they contributed by way of work? Or would it be fairer if everyone were allowed to earn and keep as much as they could? Should important decisions be taken by everyone, or only by those whose experience and knowledge best qualifies them to decide? These are fundamental questions – not about how society *actually* operates, but about how it *should* operate.

It is equally important to appreciate what political philosophy is not. It is not concerned with describing actual political societies or institutions: that is the study of politics. Nor is it the study of the way in which nations and empires have developed and spread globally: that is the study of political geography (although a knowledge of politics and political geography is useful for anyone interested in political philosophy). Nor is it the study of how finance, trade and the markets shape society: that is economics. Rather, *political philosophy is concerned with the rational and normative justification of political entities*.

Political entities?

Well, yes – because 'the political' is not simply limited to what happens at a national level. International bodies are equally relevant, as may be local groups, city states, trade unions, international companies, trading systems, shareholders and directors of companies, and even families. You could argue that 'political' can apply to all those situations where groups of people organize themselves for mutual support or action – though this is a contentious view.

Politics itself can be a practical, mechanical business – sorting out how best to deliver agreed benefits and so on. However, if it were only that, there would be few political issues to discuss – every form of government would be judged simply on the basis of its efficient delivery. But life is not that straightforward. People disagree about the principles upon which society should be run – and it is these disagreements about principles that form the basis of political philosophy.

An historical perspective

Ancient Greece and the medieval world

As exemplified by Plato and Aristotle, the political philosophy of ancient Greece addressed the issue of the good life and how it might be lived in society. Against a range of political structures of their day, they sought to root politics in metaphysics – in other words, in a fundamental understanding of the nature of humankind and the end or purpose of life. This was later taken up in a religious context, with the idea that the right form of government was one that reflected the natural order itself, as created by God, establishing a medieval hierarchy for earth and heaven. But in Renaissance Italy, conflicts between city-states, and the intrigues of political life, suggested that there were occasions when cunning, rather than godly obedience, might prevail.

Thinkers here include: Plato, Aristotle, Augustine and Machiavelli.

The rise of the individual

Following the Reformation and the English Civil War, the seventeenth and eighteenth centuries saw the development of a very different approach to politics. This is the period in which the wishes of the individual became paramount, and political structures were justified on a basis of a social contract or agreement between individuals. Rights and freedoms were debated, the French had a revolution and the American colonies broke away from British control. The end of that period also saw the rise of utilitarianism as an ethical philosophy, which resulted in political systems being judged according to their ability to deliver the greatest benefit to the greatest number of citizens. This led to the development of democracy. The question was no longer about the fundamental essence of humankind, but about the best way to organize our society.

Thinkers here include: Hobbes, Locke, Rousseau, Hume, Burke and Paine.

The evolution of systems

General systems of thought tend to create political philosophies as part of their overall understanding of reality. Kant, for example, produced rational principles for judging right and wrong, independent of anticipated results, inclinations or individual wishes. His famous 'categorical imperatives' – that something is only right if one could wish everyone else to adopt the same principle of action, that people should be treated as ends and never only as means, and that we should behave as though legislating for a kingdom in which everyone is an autonomous and free human being – have huge political implications. Hegel explored the idea that society was constantly changing in a dialectical process, and Marx took this idea up and formulated his concept of 'dialectical materialism' in which political change comes by way of class struggle. You also had the impact of Darwin and the idea of evolution through natural selection, and the attack on democracy by Nietzsche, who saw it as supporting the weak at the expense of the strong. And, at the other extreme, Mill developed the implications of utilitarianism, and argued for liberal values and freedom. By the end of the nineteenth century there was a huge range of political systems of thought.

Thinkers here include: Kant, Hegel, Marx, Mill and Nietzsche.

The twentieth-century clash of ideologies

The traumas of the twentieth century concern the clash of political ideologies that have deep roots in political philosophy. There was the massive rise and fall of communism, the challenge of fascism in Italy and Germany, and the steady global growth of democracy, riding on the back of capitalist economics. Millions died in that troubled century for the sake of political ideologies. But during much of that time political philosophy was in the doldrums. Like ethics, it came under the criticism that normative judgements (saying that something is right or wrong) were meaningless, because they could not be justified on the basis of facts. Hence, for some years, much political philosophy simply explored the origins of political structures and the meaning of key terms, without working from normative first principles. There were exceptions, of course, including those mentioned below, who challenged ideologies.

Thinkers here include: Berlin, Hayek and Popper.

The later twentieth century and the dominance of liberal democracy

By the last three decades of the twentieth century, there was a progressive decline in socialism and communism, with the liberal democratic tradition in a position of dominance. Political philosophy was revived, largely as the result of the work of John Rawls, whose seminal *A Theory of Justice* challenged utilitarian assumptions and re-instated normative philosophy to the political process. The rise of feminism questioned the male-dominated philosophy and politics of the past, and along with it normative assumptions about the purpose of life and what constitutes fairness in society. There was also discussion about the scope of 'the political', the relationship of ideas to power, the nature of rights, the existential implications of politics and the need to explore new patterns of work and living.

Thinkers here include: Rawls, Nozick, Dworkin, Habermas, Arendt, Foucault, Oakeshott, Sartre and Gorz.

The agenda continues to change, and the twenty-first century has thrown up a whole new range of issues, from terrorism to global markets, to the power of the internet, to the environment. But first let us be clear about the function of political philosophy with regard to that agenda.

Justification, not just clarification

Some see philosophy's main task as clarifying concepts. That would imply that the task of philosophy is to look at the key ideas in political debate – freedom, rights, justice, democracy, and so on – and to examine what people really mean by them, and how they are related to one another. That is the sort of philosophy that clears the mind but does not necessarily change the world.

But there is another tradition of political philosophy. Marx famously declared that he wanted to change the world, rather than just interpret it, and many other political thinkers have impacted on the course of history. Rousseau's writings were to influence the French Revolution and Locke's the American Declaration of Independence. Nietzsche's work was read by Mussolini and Hitler (and sadly misused by them), and socialist ideas lay behind the setting up of the welfare state and health service in Britain. Until recently, neo-conservative views in the United States influenced, among other things, American foreign policy with respect to the Middle East and the Iraq War. Discussions about terrorism and how to resist it are not just about words, but are desperately important in terms of security and human rights. So political concepts are not just there to be clarified, they also need to be examined and challenged.

Political ideas are potent; but are they valid? The only way to establish that is by taking a two-stage look at them. First of all they need to be clarified: What exactly do we mean by fairness, or equality, or democracy? But secondly, they need to be justified: On what basis can you argue for the fairness of this or that political system? On what basis can you justify taking military action?

The modern agenda

Political philosophy has changed considerably during the last 40 years. Before the 1970s most political philosophy involved looking at constitutions, how they were justified and how well they served to benefit the lives of citizens. After that time, the focus tended to shift towards key concepts such as:

* freedom
* justice
* equality of opportunity
* rights
* fairness in sharing material resources
* political authority and security.

In other words, the focus changed from the political structures within which people live, to those things that the individual might justly expect the state to provide or to facilitate.

But the problem is that these concepts may compete with one another. If everyone were given complete freedom, there might be no justice or fair sharing. If everyone were forced to be equal, and to receive a fixed share of material goods, individual freedom to improve one's situation in life would be curtailed. What one person may see as justice and fairness, another may see as an infringement of his or her individual rights.

A key feature of political philosophy is negotiating between these principles, and getting them to interlock for maximum benefit. But 'maximum benefit' suggests some form of distributive justice – in other words, that society should be so organized that everyone receives a fair and appropriate share of resources. For some, that economic agenda remains central to the task of political philosophy.

With the twenty-first century there arrived issues that were not on the radar in earlier times. The last two decades of the twentieth century saw the progressive failure of socialist and communist regimes, leaving the United States of America as the sole superpower. Liberal democracy and capitalism seemed to have become the only viable political and economic option. Indeed Francis Fukuyama, in his book *The End of History and the Last Man* (1992) argued persuasively that there was a universal desire for the freedoms and benefits of modern western society, and this implied that the liberal-democratic view, in the form of individual freedom and free-market economics, would be the destination of choice for everyone. That view was reflected in the 'neo-conservative' agenda in the USA, which we shall need to consider later.

To some, there is nothing more to discuss – the old Soviet-style planned economies have failed, labour and socialist parties have opted for the centre ground, and liberal democracy and free-market economics have triumphed. The sole criteria for political success are an ever-increasing standard of living and the provision of more and more consumer goods within secure national borders. All a government needs to do is adopt the policies that deliver on its economic promises.

But there are other huge issues to be addressed within the modern world. With global communication and economic structures, we have the issue of the relationship of individual nation states and international bodies. Post-colonial issues for the developing world, and multicultural ones in the developed world, both cut across the traditional national and cultural boundaries. These concerns include:

* civil rights
* feminist thinking
* globalization
* international responsibility – both in terms of war and the environment
* religious elements in political divisions
* climate change and political ecology
* terrorism.

These newer issues cannot be dealt with simply in terms of the older discussions between socialist and capitalist priorities. The rising threats to the newly-dominant, liberal-democratic view of society come from exactly those groups who reject the individual-centred philosophies of the social contract and utilitarianism, handed down from the period of the seventeenth to nineteenth centuries, in favour of submission to a larger sense of purpose and meaning, whether religious or cultural.

But to the more profound question 'What is life for?' the suicide bomber, the aid worker and the venture capitalist may have very different answers. Political philosophy itself depends on establishing at least some basic answer to that question, for without that there is nothing to counter the accusations that money and power rule over reason and principle in the political sphere, and it makes little sense to discuss the rights and wrongs of political organizations and actions.

2

looking for the good life

Fundamental to any political philosophy is the question of the good life. The philosophers of ancient Greece recognised that people needed to band together in order to achieve what they could not as individuals – security, mutual support and participation in society. Both Plato and Aristotle regarded human life as essentially political and the city-state as a necessary vehicle within which people could develop and exercise personal virtues.

In this chapter we shall look at some aspects of the political thinking of Plato and Aristotle and then turn to the Cynics, Stoics and Epicureans who followed them, but for whom the interests of the individual tended to take precedence.

Other visions of the good life were displayed by religious thinkers in the medieval period. We take a brief look at St Augustine and then move on to two very different views of political life – the power politics of Machiavelli and the utopian dreams of Sir Thomas More.

Some conception of what the good life is about is fundamental to political philosophy. When people speak about fairness, or equality, or justice, they do so because they want people to be treated properly, and given the possibility of living well. The basic question for political philosophy is this: *What sort of political structure will enable people to live well?*

If we do not know what it means to live well, if we have no idea about those things that enable people to live life to their greatest possible capacity, then we have no hope or basis of assessing the political aspects of life – because politics is not an end in itself, but a means to an end, and that end is the good life.

Why ancient Greece?

Like so much else in Western philosophy, the agenda for later debates was set in ancient Greece. Then the fundamental questions were: 'How can we live the good life?' and 'How should we organize our civic life?' These were asked against a background of small city-states – some democracies, some oligarchies, some ruled by tyrants. Their world was very different from ours, but many of the issues with which they battled remain with us to this day.

The classical period of Greek political thought, represented by the work of Plato (428–348) and Aristotle (384–322), ran from the early fifth to the late fourth centuries BCE. By that time, Greece had established itself into about 750 self-governing city-states. Each *polis*, as these were called (from which we get the term 'politics') had its own particular form of government. Most were very small, many having fewer than 1,000 citizens, but the largest – Athens – had 45,000 citizens. These *poleis* had been in existence for up to 400 years before the classical period, so Plato and Aristotle were not devising some new theory of politics, but were putting together a logical justification for political structures that had been around for a considerable time. In addition, as we shall see, Plato in particular was trying to link the structures of political life to his overall view of the world, and of the place of reason within it.

The last 30 years of the fifth century BCE had been a time of considerable bloodshed and violence. The Peloponnesian War of 431–404 BCE came to an end with the defeat of Athens at the hands of Sparta, when its democracy was overthrown and replaced by the rule of the Thirty Tyrants (which was backed by the Spartans, and led by Plato's cousin, Critas). Political opponents were executed, free speech was restricted and all who appeared to challenge or threaten the political status quo were punished. The Tyrants were overthrown the following year and democracy reinstated, but that did not imply total freedom of thought or speech – Socrates managed to survive the rule of the Tyrants, only to be put on trial and executed four years later for challenging established ideas.

It was not a time of idyllic peace and simplicity, but one that was as ruthless and unpredictable as any modern era.

Both Plato and Aristotle argued that the *polis* was needed because people were not self-sufficient, and that some things could only be achieved communally. At the same time, both felt that political life was a natural function of humankind – reading these writers, there is never a sense that one can opt to be a lone individual, separated off from others. And, if there was a major distinction to be made between nature (*physis*) and law (*nomos*), it was that man-made laws should be rooted in the nature of humankind.

Political life was life in the *polis*. It was not a separate option for professional politicians, which the ordinary person (following a personal and economic agenda) took an interest in only when he or she was directly affected. Rather, political involvement was implicit in civilized living, not an optional extra, and Aristotle (*Politics*, 1.2.1253) said that the person who lived separate from a *polis* was either a beast or a god.

However, Athens was also concerned to protect individuals, allowing them basic freedoms and also giving them protection from undue interference from agents of the *polis*. But it was clear that individual citizens could only flourish if the *polis* within which they lived was stable and secure – all were bound together, with responsibilities towards the welfare of one another. Indeed, for

Aristotle, shared activity and goals were a route towards personal happiness and fulfilment.

Political life was closely bound up with the idea of virtues. These were not simply private moral values, but those qualities without which it was not possible to live and flourish within a *polis*. The Athenians were therefore willing to define the qualities that made for a good citizen and people were encouraged to participate politically on the grounds that the *polis* provided the context for living the good life.

Political animals

If human beings are fundamentally political animals, as Aristotle suggested, then engaging in politics is absolutely natural, and attempting to live as an isolated individual is unnatural. Qualities such as respect for others and the quest for justice are therefore not arbitrary and optional extras, but express something fundamental to human life, something without which we are in danger of becoming sub-human.

Socrates is credited with saying that 'the unexamined life is not worth living', but it was equally true that – as far as qualified adult males were concerned – the non-political life was equally not worth living.

Necessary virtues

Protagoras – the first political theorist – was a sophist, whose thoughts are known through Plato's dialogue that is named after him. He offers a myth for the origins of politics – namely that when people gathered together to form societies, they generally failed because of human violence towards one another, but the gods provided two virtues to enable society to work:

* *Aidos* – moderation and respect for others
* *Dike* – justice.

Political wisdom, he argued, springs from these two virtues, which every citizen should possess, on pain of death, and which they should teach to their sons. And it is the personal qualities of moderation and respect for others that, when combined with justice – the term that Plato seeks to define in *The Republic* – is at the heart of the attempt to establish a society that is both fair and equal in its treatment of citizens.

Plato

Plato's political views are to be found in *Gorgias* and in his late works, *The Statesman* and *Laws*, but by far his best-known work and the key to his philosophy is *The Republic*. This book, like his other works, is set out in dialogue form, with Socrates debating the nature of justice with a range of characters who represent the various political viewpoints. It is very readable, and touches on so many philosophical issues that it is an ideal starting point not just for a study of political philosophy, but for philosophy in general.

What is justice?

In the dialogue, various options are presented. The debate opens by Thrasymachus arguing that justice is whatever is in the interests of the stronger – a view that remains popular today, and leads ultimately to a cynical rejection of the whole political process. This is rejected in the dialogue by Socrates (through whose mouth Plato expounds his own philosophy). He recognizes the deeply selfish elements in human nature – as illustrated by the myth of the ring of Gyges. Armed with a ring that makes him invisible and thereby free to do whatever he likes, Gyges seduces the queen, kills the king and takes over the throne. It suggests that, given the opportunity to behave with impunity, people will be motivated by their own selfish interests. What Plato wants is to offer a higher vision of ethics and the political virtues.

Another argument, put forward in *The Republic* by Glaucon, is that human nature needs to be restrained for the general benefit of society. In other words, there needs to be an agreement to prevent harm by restraining self-interest. In this, Plato anticipates the whole 'social contract' basis of political philosophy, but again he sees it as inadequate.

His own view comes in an extended exploration of the nature of the self and of the state. He describes three aspects of human beings: the appetites, the spirit or directing element, and reason. His ideal for the human being is a situation where reason rules over spirit and appetite. And this, of course, links reason with his whole notion of the best form of life – if virtue and knowledge are one and the same, then a life ruled by reason will also be the most virtuous.

In the same way, he argues that there are three classes of people in the state: the workers (corresponding to the physical appetites), those whose role it is to defend the state (corresponding to the spirited element) and finally the philosophers (reason). He argues that justice is done when each part of society is treated correctly according to its nature, and hence – since an individual is best ruled by reason – the state should be ruled by Guardians who are trained as philosophers.

Plato is effectively trying to explain the value of justice to those, like Thrasymachus, who see it as an inconvenience, or as a set of rules to be avoided if possible, while striving to benefit themselves. What he tries to show, by making the analogy with parts of the self, is that justice is essential for human flourishing, even within the self, quite apart from its effect on other people.

In *The Republic* Plato rejected various political options:

* Tyranny, because a single person, although perhaps initially representing and appealing to the ordinary people, may become corrupted by power.
* Timocracy (rule by the most powerful), because those who are in power because of their status are liable to be aggressive and more likely to declare war.
* Oligarchy (rule by a wealthy or privileged elite), because it is likely to encourage huge differences between rich and poor.
* Democracy, because it tends to anarchy.

In his critiques of these options, he tries to balance the need for stability and insight into the best way to run society, with a recognition that people tend to go for what is in their own interests, and that most of these forms of government are in danger of favouring those by whose power they have been set up.

Plato's option, of course, is that the ideal state should be run by Guardians who are philosophers, motivated by insight and reason and immune from selfish concerns.

The chief aim of Plato's *Republic* is the production of excellence: breeding couples are selected for maximum quality of offspring and those born imperfect are left to die. It is a society ruled by a carefully groomed and trained elite. But however much the prevailing liberal-democratic sensibilities of the modern political world may find Plato's ideas offensive at times, they offer an interesting challenge.

Plato's system overcomes the danger that rulers with one-sided or biased views will be elected on the basis of promises that they cannot keep. If every ruler were free from family or other partisan ties, unconcerned about personal wealth or prestige, no doubt their choices would be the most wise and beneficial. *But would you want to live in a paternalistic society, where an intellectual elite condescend to stoop to organize the political regime along lines reasoned out with disinterested precision?*

Aristotle's political options

Aristotle's political philosophy is set out in his *Nicomachean Ethics* and *Politics*. In *Politics*, he asks why it is that political institutions come about in the first place. He recognizes the need for people to band together to help secure the necessities of life, but he considers that the state is one step beyond that, in that it is basically an association of kinship groups and villages who come together in order to establish a constitution that would allow them to live *the best life possible*. In other words, rather like utilitarian ethical arguments, people bind themselves to one another because they are looking for the greatest benefit for the greatest number, and find this in some form of political constitution, offering peace and a measure of protection. For him, therefore, human beings are, by their very nature, political. His goal, *eudaimonia* (poorly translated as 'happiness', but really embracing the general sense of living and acting well), involved choosing to live as part of society. To reject society was to revert to the life of beasts. Only in participation can the individual fully realize his (not 'her' unfortunately) potential.

Aristotle carried out a survey of the various forms of political organization to be found in his day and assessed their value. He was critical of those states where power was in the hands of one person (a tyranny) or a few people (an oligarchy), or even the rule of the mob, which is how he viewed democracies. He favoured those that were monarchies, aristocracies or polities. Although noting the difference between rule by a single person, a small number or by the majority, he also considered that it was more important to see *on whose behalf* the government operated. If on behalf of the majority of citizens, it met his approval; if on behalf of a minority or an elite, he saw it as perverted.

His last option – a 'polity' – describes a political situation where everyone can participate in the decision-making process, but only a few would actually take responsibility for ruling. His 'polity' came closer to what we would now think of as representative democracy, than does 'democracy', which in his day implied rule by the whole *polis*. Like Plato, he had no illusions about the inability of most people to make informed political choices. For Aristotle, man is both a rational and a political animal, and his aim (like that of Plato) is to apply reason to issues of political rule.

In *Politics*, Aristotle criticizes militaristic states with imperialist intentions to increase their land and power, on the grounds that they actually undermine themselves, because they encourage similar traits in their citizens, who want to gain as much power and influence as they can. Hence they breed instability and discontent. This he contrasts with a state that allows and encourages freedom and participation, where citizens are willing to serve in the army to defend the state, on the basis that they feel they have a stake in it.

Aristotle thus argues for a partnership between ruler and ruled, recognizing that rule can be imposed on people for only so long before they will want to rebel. Hence, he is putting forward what amounts to a *consent-based* approach to government.

And that consent-based approach represents the balance between the potential anarchy of a direct democracy and the inflexibility of a rigid monarchy or military dictatorship. Such choices were very relevant in Aristotle's own day, and they remain so now. Stability in government depends on the consent of the people.

Cynics, Stoics and Epicureans

After the classical period of Plato and Aristotle, there was a shift of focus away from the city-state, and towards the individual. Three groups of thinkers are relevant here: the Cynics, the Stoics and the Epicureans.

Diogenes of Sinope (400–325 BCE), most famous for sleeping in a barrel and having no more possessions than he could carry, rejected the conventions of social and political life, and was therefore called a 'cynic' – in other words, he was 'like a dog'. Until then, belonging to a *polis* was assumed to be essential – it gave you status, citizenship and protection. But Diogenes, when asked to which *polis* he belonged, replied that the world (*cosmos*) was his *polis*; hence he may be seen as the first *cosmopolitan* man. That was a remarkable view to take at the time, although, to be fair, Diogenes probably presented it in rather a negative way, as rejecting the limitations of a single *polis*, rather than embracing cosmopolitanism as global citizenship. But his view reflects a shift away from seeing the individual as part of the state, to seeing the state as an option imposed on an otherwise free individual.

The Cynics, in rejecting social conventions, were precursors of modern anarchists. They saw politics as, if anything, a hindrance to living the good life, and delighted in flouting the accepted norms of their day. Stoics, on the other hand (e.g. Seneca and Marcus Aurelius) tended to be more moderate in their views, although maintaining the value and significance of the individual.

The Stoics taught that one should live in conformity with the *logos*, or rational principle within everything. In this, they were not far removed from Aristotle's view that everything had a purpose or 'end', and that its good came in fulfilling itself. Some Stoics, like

Leabharlann 21
Chontae Ceatharlach

Zeno (332–265 BCE), tended to side against conformity to laws, while others, like Cicero (106–43 BCE), were more concerned to argue for balance and the need for people to work together for the common good. But politically they emphasized the individual and his or her personal integrity. In particular the *Meditations* of Marcus Aurelius (121–80 BCE), although a set of personal reflections rather than a systematic work of philosophy, give the most direct insight into the Stoic view, and in particular the view of someone who achieves high political office – in his case, Roman emperor.

The other group of thinkers to mention here are the Epicureans. They held that the world was an impersonal place, indifferent to human welfare, and that it was up to individuals to seek their own happiness. They sought this in simplicity of living, rather than extravagance, and gathered together to share a communal life with those who held similar views.

Although fascinating, there is no scope here to explore the thinking of these groups; they are mentioned only to make a single point – that even among the thinkers of ancient Greece and Rome, there was a choice between the more centralized view of politics and the more individualistic. *Does the state exist for the sake of the individual, or the individual for the sake of the state?*

Medieval otherworldliness

In political philosophy, it may be tempting to jump straight from the work of Plato and Aristotle to the seventeenth- and eighteenth-century thinkers (like Hobbes and Locke) whose ideas have been directly influential on modern political developments. However, there are two other perspectives that need to be taken into account – one is the impact of the Christian religion on political thought, and the other is the revival of the small-scale political entity in the cities of Renaissance Italy.

The religious perspective is well illustrated by St Augustine's *City of God*. Augustine (354–430) made the clear distinction between the worldly city (the City of Man) and the heavenly abode of the faithful (the City of God). His argument was that people live in two worlds, with two sets of commitments, but that the earthly ones were of little value when compared to the heavenly. Therefore, the devout should not set great store by politics, and the only function they required of the state was that of protection – although even that was doomed to failure, because sinful human nature always led to strife.

One of the key questions during the medieval period, therefore, was the relationship between the Church and the state – between heaven and earth. It was believed that God had ordered and established society, and provided for it to be guided by the Church. Hence the devout were expected to accept the established secular authorities. The divine right of kings was part of that structure – the king ruling by the authority of God. It is also important to recognize that, as far as Europe was concerned, the Church had an authority that transcended the particular nation or monarchy. Rather than political authority being established by and for the people, you have authority being handed down from above – from God, via the Church and its approved secular rulers, to the people.

In the thirteenth century the writings of Aristotle were once again being studied, taught in newly established universities, and intellectual life was able to question political and religious authority. Seeking to combine the philosophy of Aristotle with Church teaching, Thomas Aquinas (1225–74) took a positive view of politics and law, because he believed that God had provided humankind with reason, and permitted secular authority to act on his behalf. However, the law should be 'natural law' – in other words, based on nature as interpreted by reason – and if the secular law was at odds with natural law, then the latter should take precedence. Thus the hierarchy was clearly established that the Law of God took precedence over the laws of man.

Overall, however, Aquinas took a more positive view of the secular realm than did Augustine. He even argued that the discipline of obeying the law, even if only from fear of punishment, had value, as it could lead both to peace and to the development of virtue.

Renaissance realism and principled dreaming

For an utterly different approach to political philosophy, we can turn to a writer whose cynical observations of the power politics of Renaissance Italy led his name to become synonymous with political intrigue – Niccolo Machiavelli (1469–1527).

Having spent his life in the political circles of his native Florence, close to the seat of power, Machiavelli wrote *The Prince*, which appears to be a handbook for the aspiring leader – setting out the best policies for holding together a state and increasing its power and authority. He shows that there are times when a ruthless but decisive ruler is more effectively able to control and benefit a nation than a more gentle but indecisive one.

Machiavelli is readable and stimulating, and he has that unusual quality of combining a serious and reasoned argument with wry observations of actual life and situations. How far he was making serious suggestions, and how far irony was his main weapon, is a matter for debate; his lively mind is not. *The Prince* is a great book of political philosophy, because it sets out its goals, looks at what is required to fulfil them, and then looks at the principles involved in doing so. It is realistic, rather than utopian.

In terms of political philosophy, Machiavelli sees maintaining the security and integrity of the state as paramount. All else in terms of ethical or political theory takes second place. If it is necessary to be harsh, cruel even, in order to maintain security, Machiavelli sees it as the right thing to do.

In particular, Machiavelli's advice requires that a ruler should be flexible, and should learn to anticipate the actions of others and respond accordingly. In particular, his view is one that is always pragmatic – know what you seek to achieve and then find the most effective way of achieving it. When others are crafty, adherence to absolute moral or political principles is a hindrance to maintaining one's position.

While Machiavelli was plotting success in Italy, Sir Thomas More (1478–1535) was rising through the English political ranks to become Lord Chancellor to Henry VIII. As a scholar and humanist, he was a very principled man, and paid for it with his life – for, having opposed the king's right to make himself head of the Church in England, he was executed for treason.

His *Utopia* is a wonderful book which, in fictional form, tells of an account of a far-off island, named Utopia, and established that name as a term for a social and political ideal. On the island of Utopia, small self-governing cities trade with one another and people only work as much as is needed to provide the necessities of life. All are equally responsible for getting work done and, with no hangers-on in the form of priests or aristocrats, each person's share of work is modest. All, both men and women, are equal, and gold and silver are treated as worthless, thus avoiding avarice and economic competition, but allowing public heaps of gold to be used to pay mercenaries to take care of external defence.

In many ways it is a vision of a socialist state, utterly different from the Tudor monarchy, but More insists he isn't making what could be seen as political proposals. What he sets down is simply an account of what has been described to him about a far-off place, and he comments that some of the ideas appear strange, even ridiculous.

Machiavelli's *The Prince* was written in 1514, and More's *Utopia* in 1516. Both are enjoyably readable books, from minds that sought to make sense of the political intrigues, possibilities and principles of their day. They raise political questions that are still relevant and which form an interesting historical backdrop to the flurry of new political philosophy that arose in the seventeenth and eighteenth centuries.

3

the social contract

There is a difference between power and authority: anyone with power can force compliance – as is clear from dictatorships, nations ruled by the military, or places where tribal leaders or war lords have effective control of a population. But power alone does not give a ruler legitimate authority; for that we expect the support of the people through some form of democracy.

We can therefore ask: By what right do governments rule? Why should we obey them? And if they do not reflect our wishes, should we, as a people, be free to change them? These questions, at the very heart of democracy, were debated extensively during the seventeenth and eighteenth centuries – and in this chapter we shall take a look at three thinkers from that period: Hobbes, Locke and Rousseau. Their arguments reflect the political situation of their own day, but they have been hugely influential in shaping modern ideas of democracy.

Anybody can force someone to do something by threatening to use power against them. But that does not mean that the person has 'authority' to do so. *Authority implies agreed legitimacy*. A law or an action is politically authorized if, and only if, it has the backing of a legitimately established government, and one way of establishing that legitimacy is to base it on an agreed contract made between people and their rulers – the social contract.

The idea of the political contract has a long history. In his dialogue *Crito*, Plato puts forward the argument that, by choosing to live in Athens and accepting its protection and the benefits it offers, one is obliged in return to obey its laws. He has Socrates argue that, if a person does not want to obey the laws in Athens, he should go and live elsewhere.

But the renewed interest in contract came about because, with the new thinking produced during the Renaissance, and the upheavals in Europe caused by the Reformation, there emerged a society in which emphasis was increasingly placed on the individual. Rather than seeing society as a God-given structure within which individuals were required to fit, thus fulfilling their purpose within the whole, there was a view that people should be able to get together and take their own responsibility for the political rules under which they should live.

Thus we arrive at seventeenth- and eighteenth-century **contractarianism** – in other words, the attempt to find a rational justification for the modern nation-state, based on the agreement of the people. This period set the foundations of modern democracy and liberalism – and thus forms the basis of modern political thought.

Key questions to ask about representation and consent are:
* Does this government represent me fairly?
* How do I give (or withhold) my consent for it to act in my name?
* Am I considered to have given my consent to a nation's political system simply by being born there? If not, at what point am I asked for my consent?
* What if I belong to a minority and all political decisions are made in favour of the majority? Does that mean that

I will never be treated fairly (from my perspective) in a
  democratic system?

Today, most people favour some form of democracy – that
people should agree together to support a government, rather
than having one imposed on them. That has come about, to a
considerable extent, through the work of thinkers who supported
the idea of a social contract – including Hobbes, Locke and
Rousseau.

Hobbes: an alternative to chaos

When a nation restricts civil liberties or the free flow of
information in the name of security, when it become defensive,
when it insists on maintaining tight border controls to defend itself
against terrorist threats or illegal immigrants, or when it claims
absolute authority, it follows a line of reasoning that goes back to
Thomas Hobbes (1588–1679).

Hobbes wrote at a time of political conflict – the civil war in
England, the challenge to royal authority, the execution of Charles I
and the setting up of the Commonwealth. Hobbes favoured the
monarchy, and was forced to flee to France in 1640. His best-known
work, *Leviathan* (1651) – the title of which refers to the state, named
after the great beast in the Book of Job, whose magnificence quelled
all questioning – reflects his view of the authority of the monarchy.
The charge against the king, at his trial in 1649, was that he claimed
'an unlimited and tyrannical power to rule according to his will, and
to overthrow the rights and liberties of the people of England'.

So the key questions for Hobbes concern how and why a
government is established, and what authority it should be given.

Understandably perhaps, he holds a rather bleak view of
human life and of the potential of society to descend into chaos
and bloodshed. He thinks that most human behaviour is motivated
by desires that lead to conflicts of interest and therefore disputes.
He assumes that mutual agreement alone would not be sufficient
to settle such disputes, unless there were to be some overall
authority to enforce compliance.

Therefore, the only hope for protection in a dangerous world is to band together, to set up a powerful ruler or government, and to agree to be committed to its authority. Failure to secure such an authority leaves people vulnerable to a basic trait of human nature, namely that everyone is going to be out for him or herself. In such circumstances, few will have the trust required for projects, like trade and education, that require co-operation. He famously described life for humankind in its natural state as 'solitary, poor, nasty, brutish and short', lacking all that makes for civilized living, trade, learning and so on. And just as, in the earlier 'natural law' approach, the first natural right of every human being is self-preservation, so the first duty of the state is to protect against threats to life, both internal and external.

State power is legitimized by being set up by the agreement of the people, for their mutual support and protection. The key thing to appreciate about Hobbes's main argument, however, is that authority is *given* to the ruler, rather than just *loaned*. Individual wills are given up in favour of the single sovereign will.

But the problem with this is that, once set up between individuals, the sovereign power does not have an on-going agreement with each of the citizens, but has absolute and unchallengeable authority. Of course, given Hobbes's background, that would seem perfectly reasonable, for once the sovereign power is open to challenge, each and every citizen may start to doubt its authority and refuse its laws – and you are back on the slope down to anarchy and civil strife.

The main argument against Hobbes is that his social contract does not make a government sufficiently accountable for its subsequent actions. But he adds one qualification, to use his phrase, 'except where my life is threatened'. This would suggest that, in extreme circumstances, authority is not simply *given*, but is *loaned* and the condition of that loan is that the government provides security. Given that Hobbes's whole purpose is to establish an authority that provides security and avoids anarchy, this is reasonable. Hobbes allows people to rebel, but only if absolutely necessary in order to protect themselves.

Locke and the principles of democracy

John Locke (1632–1704) welcomed the 'glorious revolution' of 1688, when William of Orange arrived in England to establish a constitutional monarchy, and James II emigrated to France, thus showing that it was possible to remove and replace a ruler without bloodshed or national trauma, in stark contrast to the upheavals of the civil war earlier in the century. His *Second Treatise on Civil Government* (1689) was a justification of that new political situation – a triumph of compromise that would establish a monarchy and strong leadership, but allow control to remain in the hands of the people.

In Locke's work we find much that has contributed to the modern liberal democratic tradition, and his ideas were to influence both the French and American constitutions. The reason why Locke is crucial in political philosophy is that he argued for representation in government, with ways of ensuring that governments are held to account.

Key to Locke's argument is that a government should establish laws by consent of the people, and should then be held accountable, so that no ruler can be *above* the law. Hence the institutions of government are agencies for the implementing of law, rather than having absolute power to make and change the law. This is what distinguishes Locke's position from that of Hobbes.

Locke was not as negative as Hobbes concerning the natural state. He believed that, in the absence of laws or political control, where people would be absolutely free to choose what to do, some would still be willing to work together for mutual support. However, he argued that such a state did not offer protection for a person's 'property', and thus that they would remain in fear:

> *This makes him willing to quit this condition which, however free, is full of fears and continual dangers; and it is not without reason that he seeks out and is willing to join in society with others who are already united, or have a mind to unite for the mutual preservation of their lives, liberties and estates, which I call by the general name – property.*

And he pointed out that the natural state lacked two things:

Firstly, there wants an established, settled, known law. Received and allowed by common consent to be the standard of right and wrong, and the common measure to decide all controversies between them ...

Secondly, in the state of Nature there wants a known and indifferent judge, with authority to determine all differences according to established law.

Second Treatise of Civil Government, Chapter IX

Property

Locke saw that, in a state of nature, people could hunt animals and gather food, and thereby take for themselves what would previously be regarded as common. The act of hunting had made it theirs, and they therefore considered themselves to be entitled to it. He thus established the principle that the act of labour – mixing one's own efforts with what nature provides – is the basis for property.

Though the earth and all inferior creatures be common to all men, yet every man has a 'property' in his own 'person'. This nobody has any right to but himself. The 'labour' of his body and the 'work' of his hands, we may say, are properly his. Whatsoever then he removes out of the state that nature has provided, and left it in, he hath mixed his labour with it, and joined to it something that is his own, and thereby makes it his property.

Second Treatise of Civil Government, Chapter V

For Locke, people are essentially free to take their own interests seriously; they have a right to work for and keep wealth, and if they have invested their time and energy in a project, even one that has taken natural resources that might originally have been considered to belong to everyone, then they are entitled to keep them for themselves. This right to own and defend one's property is a central feature of the freedom of the individual; the state is there to protect private interests, and to create the conditions of security that allow commerce. Naturally, the organization of defence and law requires the raising of funds through taxation, but Locke argues that this should be with the consent of the majority.

Laws and executive power

Locke also distinguishes between the legislative and executive aspects of government. The legislative side establishes the laws by which the state will be run. The executive sets about implementing them, and part of that implementation is the setting up of an impartial legal system. Hence the right of parliament to endorse or hold to account a government, and if necessary to change it. This remains an essential part of modern representative democracy. In Britain, the Prime Minister and other ministers are required to present themselves before the House of Commons to explain their actions and their proposals for legislation – and these can then be scrutinized and, if appropriate, changed, before they can become law.

Majority rule

How do you protect a minority or an individual from the wishes of the majority? And how do you establish that everyone has given consent to be governed in this way? Locke himself recognized this issue and made a distinction between consent that is given directly, in the making of an agreement, and consent that is *tacit*. Naturally enough, most people will be judged to have given tacit consent, since they have not actually been present to set up the government in the first place.

If rule is by consent, then I should be able to select and direct those who are set up to control me. But the laws are set up by the consent of the majority. How does an individual or a minority respond when the will of the majority – or at least, the government for which a majority has voted – goes against their own interests? This may be termed 'the paradox of sovereignty': that people are subject to a ruler who is actually selected to act as their own agent.

There is another fundamental problem here. The whole reason for establishing a social contract was that people, left to their own devices, could not always be trusted to keep their own contracts with one another, and hence everyone would be vulnerable to exploitation by all the others. How then can people be trusted to keep the social contract they make with the government?

The logical answer to this is that they can't. If a small number of people defy the law, they may be punished for it. If a majority complain that a law is unjust, or seek to change the government, the fact that they are a majority appears to give their action legitimacy.

Representative democracy

From simple democracy in ancient Athens, we have moved to a situation of representative democracy, necessitated by the sheer number of people involved. Hence it is clear that if representatives are to be voted into office, those voting must have a clear idea of what they will intend to do, to ensure that they will reflect the wishes of voters.

This is made more complex by the party system. Where the person standing for election belongs to a party, it is assumed that he or she will follow that party's position on the major issues under discussion. From time to time, of course, in order to represent constituents, a representative may need to go against the party line. But that is the exception rather than the rule.

It is assumed that, where a government is formed from those of a particular party who have gained a majority of seats, that government will put into effect those things that the party presented to the electorate in its campaign. Hence the government may claim to have a mandate from the electorate to put into effect the manifesto or platform upon which it campaigned.

But notice the problem this causes. In a representative democracy, only a majority of elected members need support the party which seeks to put itself forward to govern. Hence, at any one time, the government in power can, at the very most, claim to be implementing ideas voted for by a majority of the people, and it is quite likely that, for any one particular piece of legislation, it will represent only a minority view, since not every elected representative in a party will give equal support to the legislation, and not every voter who supported him or her will necessarily have approved of that aspect of the party's manifesto. Thus, unless you have a referendum on each and every piece of legislation (which would not be practicable in a modern democracy), it is impossible to know what percentage of the population actually support it.

It is also clear that, in any representative democracy which is organized along party lines, decisions about those things that fall within the responsibility of the executive, will (through a natural desire to stay in power) reflect the interests of the ruling party. This would include, for example, the decision about when to call a general election. In other words the consent and mandate of the people, which alone legitimizes those in office, can itself be timed to benefit those presently in office.

To what extent, then, should a representative democracy with a party system claim to be able to put into effect a government which accurately represents the people? And if it admits the limitations of any such process, is there any better way of operating?

Might it be possible, for example, to hold a referendum on major issues? The problem here is that the framing of the straightforward question that it puts to the electorate in a referendum is in the hands of the government – and the way the question is framed may influence the result. Hence, with the best will in the world, the process of democracy is no more than an on-balance probability that the government is putting into effect the wishes of the people.

A key question is this: If a government is elected on a mandate, and the circumstances that led to the formulation of that mandate change, is that government entitled to act differently from the way it promised the electorate? That might appeal to common sense. On the other hand, if it then acts against its own mandate, does it not become an elected dictatorship – acting against the expressed wishes of the voters?

Rousseau: the tyranny of the general will

If people were not so foolish as to walk around brandishing the latest mobile phones and iPods, there would be far less street crime, because the temptation to snatch and run would be diminished!

In essence, that was the view of Jean-Jacques Rousseau (1712–78) a philosopher and man of letters, whose personal life was remarkably colourful, and whose political and social views were to influence the French Revolution (even though he himself did not live to see it). He contrasted the natural state of humankind with the very unnatural conditions of society. In their natural state people would simply take what they needed for life, they would not be tempted to steal from others because the whole notion of private property would not exist. It is the privatizing of things that leads to social unrest.

Nevertheless, people do in fact live in society and are open to the corruption that comes with it, so how then might they regain their freedom and innocence? Are freedom and civil society compatible?

That, in effect, is the question that lies behind one of the great 'one-liners' of political philosophy, the opening of his book *The Social Contract*:

Man is born free, and everywhere he is in chains.

In *The Social Contract* he seeks to reconcile freedom and authority. He argues that one is obliged to obey the state because it represents the 'general will' – not just the will of the majority, but what everyone would *really* want, from a moral point of view, if they considered the situation rationally and took into consideration the interests of all.

Rousseau considered that, if you are enslaved by a particular interest or desire, you are not truly free, even if you are allowed to follow it. Freedom means freedom also from your own inclinations and passions. Hence Rousseau could accept that, in order to be truly free, people should obey the general will, rather than following their own untrustworthy particular wills. If everyone were wise enough, they would see that true interest and fulfilment would come by following the general will.

But here comes the catch. People are not always wise. They may not appreciate that the general will represents their own best interests. They may not appreciate that following the general will is their path to true freedom. Therefore it may be necessary for the state to force people to do what they would 'really' (if they were wiser) want in the first place. To use Rousseau's chilling phrase, they should be 'forced to be free'.

One problem with Rousseau's approach is that it assumes two things: that everyone wants the same thing – in other words, that the general will represents the self-interest of all – and that it is a moral and political obligation of every citizen to follow that imposed self-interest. But:

> * the first is, factually, impossible to establish (unless you can have a vote on every issue)
> * the second is not something that facts alone can decide; it is a matter of personal choice.

You may point out the course of action that, in your opinion, is in my best interest, but as a free individual, I should be able to decide whether I want to accept or reject your advice. To do other than that, if I have good reasons for rejecting it, is to render self-contradictory the notion that it is in fact my 'best interest' – it cannot be 'best' for me unless it is what I freely choose.

But how are people to decide on what legislation to agree on?

*Will it be by common agreement, or by sudden inspiration?
Has the body politic an organ for expressing its will? ... How
would a blind multitude, which often knows not what it
wishes because it rarely knows what is good for it, execute
of itself an enterprise so great, so difficult as a system of
legislation?*

The Social Contract, Chapter 6 (translated by H.J. Tozer)

His answer is that a superior intelligence, in the form of a wise
legislator, is needed to perform that task. Such a role is so exalted
that Rousseau sees such a person as believing himself capable
of changing human nature and 'substituting a social and moral
existence for the independent and physical existence which we
have all received from nature'. The problem is that, for their own
good, the people will need to be changed for the better. That goal,
for the best of reasons, has been the inspiration of many a dictator.

Rousseau mocked the British for being free only when they
held an election, between which times they were content to submit
to the rule of their government. That may be a valid criticism of
any representative democracy, but is it any worse than continually
being told that the government knows what you really want and
then forcing you to have it?

Still relevant?

All modern ideas about respect for the individual, equality
of opportunity, or the independence of the judiciary, for example,
assume that government is done by consent, and in a way that
satisfies the majority of citizens. Liberal democracy – now seen
by many as the only viable political ideology – finds its origins in
seventeenth-century debates. Hence, to appreciate the present,
it is important not to forget the discussions of the past.

Finally, notice the huge shift that has taken place as we move
from the ancient Greek and medieval world to the seventeenth
century. In earlier political thinking, the task was to align the
operations of society with a sense of ultimate purpose, so that
people could live the good life and flourish. It did not depend

on what individuals thought might be to their benefit, but upon a serious consideration of the purpose of life. An ideal form of government was out there to be discovered.

Now, with the theories of social contract, the emphasis has shifted to what people *want*. Whether it is the basics of democracy or utilitarianism, it is the wishes and preferences of people that count. Government is to be constructed and shaped to fit our wishes.

The problem, from the standpoint of the individual citizen, was how – once you have created your Leviathan, or your general will – you retain some sort of control over that political beast. How do you then avoid the possibility that you, as an individual, will have your freedom curtailed for the supposed benefit of the whole? Here it is Locke, rather than Hobbes or Rousseau, who provides the effective possibility of political reform: the people are in charge, and they can change a government that does not satisfy their intentions.

4

equality and fairness

People want to be treated fairly, but does that mean that everyone should be given exactly the same material goods and services? And if they were, would that make them equal? Or indeed, given people's different abilities, would they stay equal for long? Would strict economic equality stifle any incentive to work or improve oneself?

In this chapter we shall look at the moral theory of utilitarianism, as it applies to the political sphere and at capitalism as a mechanism for generating wealth, and ask how they help or hinder the quest for fairness. We shall look particularly at the work of John Rawls and his idea of justice as fairness.

And because fairness is about more than the distribution of goods, we shall need to look again at democracy and consider the extent to which a democratic system can contribute to establishing a fair and equal system for everyone in society.

Essentially, people want to feel that they are being treated fairly, for example, that they are not paying too much tax relative to what they receive back from the government. They complain if another section of the population is being given benefits that they are denied – whether it is tax incentives or social security payments – on the grounds that people should be treated *equally* and *fairly*.

There are, of course, many other ways in which people want to be treated fairly and equally, but the sharing out of material resources is a good place to start, and to do this we need to step back and look at two key features of the political landscape: utilitarianism and capitalism.

Utilitarianism and capitalism

Utilitarianism is the ethical theory based, broadly, on the idea that the right thing to do is that which offers the prospect of the greatest benefit to the greatest number of people involved. Developed by Jeremy Bentham (1748–1832) and John Stuart Mill (1806–73), it is probably the most widely used ethical theory today. There are three main forms of utilitarianism:

* act utilitarianism assesses the results of particular actions
* rule utilitarianism adds to this a consideration of the overall benefit offered to society in maintaining general rules
* preference utilitarianism requires that everyone's preferences should be taken into account – in other words, taking note of what people see as to their benefit, rather than telling them.

The 'principle of utility' therefore requires that a political system should be judged according to whether it produces more or less benefit, welfare and happiness for the greatest number of its citizens. In terms of political philosophy, utilitarianism would therefore seem to be a logical implication of democracy. If everyone can take part in electing a government, the expectation is that the government will then operate to the benefit of the majority. Indeed, that principle, although not couched in utilitarian terms, goes back to Plato and Aristotle. In a just society, it is the interests of the majority, rather than those of an elite, that should prevail.

Capitalism is generally regarded as the obvious way of delivering what a utilitarian assessment requires, and it is assumed that the task of government is to get out of the way and allow capitalist market forces to deliver the goods, providing the standard of living that people want.

Indeed, nineteenth-century utilitarianism generally held that the government should not interfere in the bargaining between workers and the owners of capital, on the grounds that a free-market economy would actually yield the greatest good for the greatest number.

Socialists might argue that industries should be nationalized, so that everyone, rather than just the shareholders, profit. On the other side, a neo-liberal or conservative view of this would be that efficiency and profit are the incentives that drive business forward, and that end up benefiting everyone involved. Both arguments are utilitarian.

Issues for utilitarianism

When we say that everyone should have the best possible health care or a reasonable standard of living in retirement, we are not making a utilitarian assessment about what would benefit society as a whole, we are making a case for what we consider to be the reasonable expectation of the individual, and what would be considered a just arrangement for society. In other words, the judgement is based on an assessment of what constitutes a civilized life for the individual. It would be right to promote such a civilized life, even if society as a *whole* did not benefit from it. *In other words, there are some basic rights that should take precedence over general benefit.* A fundamental question for utilitarianism is therefore: Do human rights trump utilitarian benefits?

Another question: How do you assess who is involved, and therefore whose interests should be taken into account? Should that be done on a local basis, or in terms of the workforce of a particular company? Should it be regional or national? Indeed, should it be global?

When it comes to global warming or restrictions on international trade, the interests of the citizens of one country may well conflict with the overall interests of the global community. Which utilitarian assessment do you take into account – the local or the global?

The other side of this coin is the complaint that, in any utilitarian assessment, minorities get trumped by majorities, and are therefore discriminated against when it comes to having their preferences taken into account.

This, of course, applies to both utilitarianism and democracy.

Issues for capitalism

Capitalism is essentially a mechanism for generating wealth, and it requires that the profit motive is primary. But unrestrained capitalism may produce results (conditions of working people, effects on the environment, etc.) that people find unacceptable. In other words, the social or environmental price of generating wealth for those who own capital may be seen as unacceptably high.

In practice then, looked at theoretically, political direction and free-market capitalism look incompatible, since the economic principles that drive capitalism are not political. However, most states feel the need to impose politically motivated legislation upon industry in the name of fairness, by anti-monopoly legislation, for example, or by rules that apply to the environmental impact of products, or their marketing (for example, restrictions on the advertising of tobacco products).

Marx thought that working people were threatened by alienation – for rather than being able to take pride in what they produced, they were reduced to cogs in an impersonal wheel of production. That is still a relevant threat, but along with it goes 'commodification' as all aspects of the individual's life is given monetary rather than personal value – from the job to the notion of fame, everything has its price and place.

But are capitalism and utilitarianism capable of achieving fairness in society, or is something more needed?

Distributive justice

It is often assumed that the key feature of good government is its management of the economy. In other words, what people want is an ever-increasing standard of living, and a government is put in power in order to deliver the goods. There are, of course, other factors – people want schools, hospitals, roads, security – but even the provision of these takes on economic and political significance, since the most wealthy are more likely to use private medicine, education and so on, whereas the poorer have no choice but to accept what the state supplies.

But how do you decide how goods should be distributed? Do you do so on the basis of:

* what people need?
* what people deserve?
* equal shares for all?

Marx held that people should give according to their ability and receive according to their needs. Is that a realistic aspiration? In terms of distributive justice, one thinker has dominated discussion for more than 30 years: John Rawls.

The revival of interest in political philosophy in recent times is often seen as having been initiated by John Rawls's book *A Theory of Justice* (1972), and his view of justice as fairness has been influential; many agree with it but equally many who see things differently have been provoked to respond to it and point out its shortcomings. Rawls wanted to show that a broadly liberal–democratic view of the distribution of resources could be given firm and logical foundations. He was also critical of the application of utilitarianism to the issue of justice and fairness.

Rawls (1921–2002) presented a 'thought experiment' in order to get to grips with the logic of any redistribution of resources. Imagine a group of people gather together to decide how resources are to be distributed (he calls this the 'original position'). Each is able to say what is in his or her own best interest, but none of them knows who they are or what their position is in society. In other words, they do not know if they themselves are rich or poor. Rawls argues that each of them, since they will not know if they are in fact the poorest in society, will not want to legislate in any way that would adversely affect themselves if that were the case. He therefore argues that such people, thinking through the logic of their position, will opt for two things:

* That each person should have equal rights to the most extensive system of liberty, provided that it does not prevent others from having similar liberties.

* That, if there are to be any inequalities in the distribution of resources, such inequalities should always be such as to benefit the least advantaged in society, and also that all should have a fair and equal opportunity to secure offices and positions.

Now there are a number of significant points to make about Rawls's argument. The first is that he clearly comes from a liberal–democratic position, seeking freedom for all, whilst maintaining social justice in the distribution of wealth. What he seeks to do in his thought experiment is to frame a logically coherent framework to support that wish.

In other words, rather as Immanuel Kant had argued that ethics should be based on pure practical reason, without any thought of personal rewards or results, so Rawls is arguing that redistributing in favour of the poorest is what everyone would see as the logical thing to want, if they were not influenced by their own social position.

But it is also important to appreciate that Rawls is concerned as much with the process by which fairness is established as about the final result. He wants to show that it is possible, through pure logic and people's natural self-interest, to establish rules for a fair distribution in society without reference to any external authority.

Rawls's criticism of utilitarianism

What Rawls offers is a form of 'ideal contractualism' – a modern version of the social contract theory of the seventeenth and eighteenth centuries – which he hoped would provide an alternative to utilitarianism. He believed that a social contract approach takes the individual more seriously than does utilitarianism, since it does not require an individual to sacrifice any benefit in favour of society as a whole. This, of course, is a major problem with utilitarianism, for majorities always seem to trump minorities.

But Rawls also felt that utilitarianism was at odds with our usual moral judgements. In other words, we have an intuitive view of what is implied by fairness which does not necessarily comply with the conclusion of a utilitarian assessment of benefits. This is a widely held criticism of act utilitarianism – that there are occasions when a weighing of the potential benefits of a course of action to all those involved does not give a result that a morally sensitive person finds acceptable.

Rawls therefore wanted to establish a 'reflective equilibrium' between the principles of justice and people's 'considered moral judgements'. He wanted his proposal for fairness to be compatible with firm moral traditions that people already hold, and he has an underlying moral assumption that individuals deserve the right to equal respect. In other words, the 'original position' is not autonomous as a way of establishing principles of justice – for it depends on prior moral positions or 'intuitions'.

R.M. Hare (1919–2002) is one of those who felt that this rigged Rawls's argument to give anti-utilitarian conclusions which Rawls himself held from the start. In other words, Rawls works on basic assumptions that are part of the modern liberal democratic tradition, and then devises an artificially contrived situation that attempts to establish them on the basis of pure logic.

Problems with Rawls's 'original position'

Here is a major problem: *Thought experiments are just that; they do not reflect what happens in real life.* There never was and never will be a situation in which people do not know their place in society, and of course Rawls never suggested that there could be. But does this attempt to construct an unreal situation in order to show the logic of self-interest give a result that can be translated into the real world? This question lies behind a criticism of Rawls from a **communitarian** standpoint.

Communitarians argue that people are always embedded in society; that we are who we are because of our place in our community, what we do, how we relate to others and so on. Hence you cannot meaningfully take from people the awareness of who they are, for that is essential for any form of political awareness and decision-taking. Hence the decisions taken by those in Rawls's 'original position' may sound logical, but they cannot reflect what actually happens when people get together.

That does not mean that people might not, for altruistic reasons, opt for a form of justice that does not benefit them personally – but if they do so, they do so with their eyes open. In actual fact, many people might want to take a risk – to opt for a situation where, if they are better off, they can benefit still further. They may reckon that the risk of losing out is worth taking. In some ways this is typical of the entrepreneur within a capitalist system, reckoning that it is better to take a risk in the hope of making a greater profit, rather than playing safe and making very little.

Hence, even if Rawls's logic is sound, it is not and can never be the sort of logic that real people in real political situations can use.

Fair opportunities

A very different approach from that of Rawls was taken by Robert Nozick in *Anarchy, State and Utopia* (1974), another hugely influential book. Nozick's view is that priority should be given to the right of individuals to generate wealth and retain it for themselves. He thinks it is wrong for the state to impose equality by taxing those who have made money in order to contribute to services for those in need. Nozick argues that it is perfectly all right to give to someone if you so choose, but not to have society force you to contribute. This, of course, reflects a strong tradition of charity giving in the USA. Where state taxation and provision are less, the opportunity for individual moral responsibility to provide for people increases.

Whereas Rawls thought that you could abstract people from their background in order to get some ideal view about principles of justice, Nozick argued that it was important to include the historical acquisition of property in assessing justice. In other words, he recognized that a key feature of a person's identity is what they possess and how they came to possess it. Also, people's abilities are linked with their background, education, opportunities in society and so on. So it is difficult to see how any justice can be established unless the economic and social background of individuals is taken into account.

Fairness is a philosophical concept based on the understanding of how the different parts of society work together, what they need, and how they can flourish. Sounds familiar? Of course – for here we are back with Plato and his threefold division of society. For all the limitations of Plato's *The Republic*, at least it recognizes that different people have different needs.

And should those who have the natural ability to succeed beyond that of their fellows be prevented from flexing their economic and political muscles? Even if all were equally provided for, they would not remain economically equal for long. Here we touch on the philosophy of Friedrich Nietzsche (1844–1900) and his sense of humankind being in the forefront of evolution, moving forward and aspiring to overcome itself, working towards the arrival of the *Übermensch* (his 'higher man' or 'superman'), who will embody the next stage of human evolution.

Absolute equality may sound fine, but how would you give people the incentive to work and contribute as much as they can, if they receive the same in return, whatever the value of their contribution? Is it natural that people should expect to receive the benefits of their contribution and consider that to be only fair?

Equality of self-direction and moral regard

Equality is a foundational concept for much political debate and political philosophy. The American Declaration of Independence of 1776 claimed 'all men are born equal' as the starting point for setting up its political system. We have already considered distributive justice as a way of treating people equally, but what else is implied by it?

There are different forms of equality:

* Equality of opportunity – even if people end up in different positions in terms of wealth and achievement, because of their differences in abilities or intelligence, they should all have the same opportunities presented to them. Thus, for example, access to schooling or job opportunities should be equally open to everyone.

* Equality of goods – this has already been considered, and suggests that people should receive an equal share of resources. In practice, of course, except in the most restricted of communities, such equality cannot be maintained for long, because people make very different uses of whatever resources they are given.

* Equality of rights – that there are basic rights offered to all alike, such as the right to life, liberty and the pursuit of happiness, or freedom from persecution on grounds of colour, race, religion and so on.

* Equality of respect – however different people may be in their abilities, they should all receive the same degree of respect, simply by being a member of the human species.

* Equality of representation – the idea that everyone should have the same opportunity to vote, or in any other way take part in the process of government. Thus, for example, members of parliament claim that they are available to all their constituencies equally. Not all will make use of that availability, but at least it is offered.

These various aspects of equality contribute to two very basic requirements for a fair and equal society – equality of *self-direction* and of *moral regard*. The first of these is the right of an individual to decide how he or she should live, and to take actions as far as possible, to put in place life-plans that aim at giving self-fulfilment.

Not all philosophers have argued for this. Aristotle claimed that women and slaves were not able to reason, or at least to reason effectively (in the case of women), and therefore they needed to be directed by men. Indeed, the thrust of his argument is that they will benefit from this, and lead happier lives, since they are supplied with an organized way of living that they would not be able to achieve if left to their own devices. This view continues to be found wherever an authority claims to know what is in the interests of an individual, even if it is not what he or she wants.

Equality of moral regard is essential for establishing a fair way of dealing with those who are most vulnerable. In considering a person's rights, and the moral obligation of society towards them, it is crucial that who they happen to be is disregarded. Hence, it should make no difference morally, whether the person under consideration is young or old, male or female, a citizen or an illegal immigrant – all should have equal moral consideration.

Another way of expressing the scope of equality within political discussion is simply to say that people should be treated with *equal consideration*.

Democracy

The term 'democracy' is derived from the Greek word *demos* (people) and *kratos* (power). It is 'people power' in the sense that people are able to choose and change a government by a process of election. Democracy would seem to be the logical expression of equality. It asserts that every adult in a society, provided that he or she qualifies in some basic way, is able to express a view about the way society is governed. Just as Bentham's principle of utility argues that the right thing to do is what offers the maximum benefit to the greatest number, so a democracy is the right form of government, according to utilitarianism, since it conforms to the wishes of the majority.

Or is it? In Aristotle's day, democracy was only for a male minority; women and slaves had no say in government. And his justification for that was simply that participation should be limited to those capable of making informed judgements, and that requires the ability to reason and a measure of financial security. Although Kant favoured democracy, he never considered that it should extend down to wage labourers, and thought that nobody should vote who did not earn his own living by business or a profession. And Nietzsche felt that democracy would hold back the development of the strong. When you consider how to wield power effectively, as described by Machiavelli in *The Prince*, you may wonder whether power is best exercised by those in the precarious situation of always being at the mercy of the people at the next election.

Plato disliked democracy because it appeared to him to be mob rule – now it has become the political option of choice. Indeed, it is often assumed that, once freed from the imposition of military or religious dictatorships, nations will automatically follow the wishes of the people and establish democracies. In practice, however, once established, democracy is carefully 'managed' by the government of the day. Voters are made promises, they are bombarded with advertisements from contending political parties, their choices are limited, and the outcome is statistically predictable, once a general tendency in voting has become apparent.

Aided by the popular press, majorities may dominate minorities, which is a clear issue for any democratic or utilitarian system. But informed agreement is equally confusing. In a modern democracy (where voting is done through the proxy of focus groups and opinion polls most of the time), the outcome of issues depends to a considerable extent on the way in which they are presented by the government, and whether there is an alternative view to be presented by opposition parties. In other words, public opinion is always open to 'spin'. Facts are more difficult to establish, and it is assumed that only a few people will know all the facts and issues on any one topic.

Governments are there to *persuade* people. If a government has a working majority, the political party providing the government need not be unduly concerned about short-term adverse poll ratings – but when these becomes sustained, or an election is approaching, is there added pressure to present and sell issues in a way that will please the electorate?

Democracy can mean many things. To Plato it was rule by an unthinking majority. To the 'social contract' proponents in the eighteenth century, it was the new voice of the people in establishing their control over government. Today, representative democracies are, in general, carefully managed, manipulated and predictable systems of government – hovering between centralized government by a professional political elite, and government by the occasional whim of a minority of people in marginal constituencies.

5

freedom

Freedom is arguably the most fundamental and crucial concept in political philosophy. It raises basic questions: What is the purpose of being free? Do I simply want all restraints removed? Should I be free to plan out my life as I wish? What should happen if my freedom clashes with that of others? Would complete freedom for all result in chaos and anarchy?

In this chapter we shall look at both the negative (freedom from) and positive (freedom to) aspects of freedom, as they were set out by the twentieth-century philosopher Isaiah Berlin, which have important implications for states that tend to be paternalist in imposing ideas of freedom.

We shall also look at the issue of free speech and at the 'harm' principle, set out by John Stuart Mill, a nineteenth-century thinker and politician, which argues that the only limitation on your freedom is that you should not harm others.

If there were no problems with freedom, there would probably be no need for political philosophy or, indeed, politics. We have an issue because it is clear that, in a complex society, people cannot simply do their own thing without recognizing that what they do impacts on others, and that they are impacted upon in return. Hence, politics is a way of negotiating between ordered constraint and freedom of the individual. The key questions are:

* How is the idea of liberty related to the need for law and for political control?
* Where is the line to be drawn between things that should be left to the individual and things where conformity to the state is the best option?

Clearly, complete freedom for everyone would lead to chaos and anarchy (in the common meaning of that term), and it would be incompatible with the complex nature of society – you cannot organize education, health care, defence, and so on, if everyone is free to do whatever they like, because all those things depend on people being predictable and conforming to basic rules to enable society to work. On the other hand, nobody would consider it right for people to behave like ants, obeying fixed rules and dedicating all their energy unthinkingly to the benefit of the colony as a whole. The severest criticism of some socialist and communist states is that they have attempted, for the general good, to deny people freedom to live as they choose. Clearly, there has to be a balance.

The basic question is simply: *Why should I accept anyone else telling me what to do? Why should I not simply do what I like?*

This leads towards a *negative* definition of freedom – in other words, freedom is what is left to you once other people's interference in your life is taken into account. In its *positive* sense, however, freedom is about choosing how to live, what to do, and the having the ability to set our own agenda and goals.

These two senses of freedom – negative freedom and positive freedom – were famously set out by Isaiah Berlin in a lecture entitled 'Two Concepts of Liberty', delivered at the University of Oxford in 1958, and itself a very good starting point for anyone interested in political philosophy.

Negative freedom

This is freedom from those things that limit what we can do. Philosophers who concentrate on this form of freedom attempt to define the minimum freedom that should be allowed to individuals in order for them to maintain their dignity as human beings. It is freedom 'from' rather than freedom 'to'.

John Stuart Mill (1806–73), whose work *On Liberty* is a key text for considering this approach to freedom, suggested that human creativity would be crushed without a suitable level of freedom. Isaiah Berlin disagreed with this, arguing that creativity can flourish even within the most repressive of regimes. This is a crucial point, because if Mill is right, then freedom 'from' restraints is absolutely essential if you are to have the freedom 'to' express and develop yourself as a creative individual. On the other hand, if Berlin is right, then an awareness of the 'freedom to' can enable positive and creative living, even in those situations where external conditions are harsh and restrictive.

Mill's 'harm' principle

Mill recognized that not every society was ready for its individual members to take responsibility for freedom in the way he was about to propose. In the case of what he calls 'backward' states:

> *Despotism is a legitimate mode of government in dealing with barbarians, provided the end be their improvement, and the means justified by actually effecting that end.*

> *Liberty, as a principle, has no application to any state of things anterior to the time when mankind have become capable of being improved by free and equal discussion.*

> from *On Liberty*

In other words, up to the point at which they can act as autonomous, thinking individuals, all that people need is a benign ruler who will tell them what to do.

How do you judge when a society or individuals within it are sufficiently mature and autonomous to accept the freedoms that Mill is about to recommend for them?

Are most people really ready to exercise their freedom responsibly? What about children, or the senile, or those with major emotional or psychological problems, or those with a very low IQ?

Mill pointed out that in ancient Greece the rulers thought it appropriate to issue guidelines for how people should behave and what they should think. Mill was against that – in a civilized society, people should be free to make up their own minds. To impose an idea on others is to assume that you are infallible, and that is simply not the case.

Contrast this with Plato, who thought that the philosophers should be able to control and tell people what to do. Plato felt that it was the responsibility of rulers to guide people to behave in a way that was to their own good.

Mill wanted to maximize freedom. He argues that:

... the only purpose for which power can be rightfully exercised over any member of a civilized community, against his will, is to prevent harm to others. His own good, either physical or moral, is not a sufficient warrant.

Because:

Over himself, over his own body and mind, the individual is sovereign.

from *On Liberty*

In other words, even if you think that it would be to someone's benefit, or long-term happiness, that they should be compelled to do something, or refrain from doing something, that is insufficient reason for interfering. Even if one can see that someone is going to harm themselves, they must not be stopped from exercising their freedom from doing so. The only limitation is that they should not be permitted to *harm* anyone else. A person should be free to plan their life to suit their own character, and have complete liberty of 'tastes and pursuits', even if others think them 'foolish, perverse, or wrong'.

On this basis, Mill argues for liberty of conscience, thought and feeling, and of expression, and also the freedom to unite together. In other words, you should be freely allowed to think, speak and act as an individual – and gather other people together to do, think or act – provided that no harm is done to others in the process.

> *The only freedom which deserves the name, is that of pursuing our own good in our own way, so long as we do not attempt to deprive others of theirs, or impede their efforts to obtain it.*
>
> from *On Liberty*

A key problem is that we often do not appreciate all the consequences of what we do. Without realizing it, our freedom may be limiting that of others. In any competitive environment, all are free to win, but when one person does so, others have their freedom to win curtailed.

Free speech

> *If all mankind minus one were of one opinion, and only one person were of the contrary opinion, mankind would be no more justified in silencing that one person than he, if he had the power, would be justified in silencing mankind.*
>
> from *On Liberty*

A key feature of Mill's view of liberty is freedom of speech, of which the quotation above is the clearest and most extreme expression. However, there are certain restraints that might be placed upon it, in the light of his 'harm' principle – since the expression of a point of view can be taken as incitement to hatred or to revolution. Hence there are restrictions on the freedom of expression devised to prevent offence being given on grounds of religion, race, gender, sexual proclivity or age.

The problem with this is to know exactly what might be deemed to cause offence or harm. What about humour or irony? Can a comedian not make reference to religion, gender, sex, race or age in a joke? Is the intention as important as the words used?

Objections to Mill

There are at least two fundamental objections to Mill's view of the freedoms that should be permitted to individuals. The first is:

* That every action may have an effect on others, even if we are quite unaware of what that effect might be. In other words, it is naive of him to assume that what I do in the privacy of my own home is not of immediate concern to other people.

To take an extreme example, downloading child pornography is done privately, and it can be argued that the material is already available on the web, waiting to be purchased, and therefore the act of making any particular download does not materially harm anyone. Now the act of downloading might not affect anybody else, but it is regarded as a serious criminal offence, because the trade in child pornography is based on the sexual exploitation of children. The person who downloads the result is therefore implicated in its production, and therefore in the prior harm done to those children. In the same way, the private act of taking illegal drugs cannot be separated from the harm that may be caused to others through the exploitative nature of the drugs trade.

Hence, although those acts appear to be done in private, Mill's argument would still condemn them on the basis of the prior harms done. This does not deny that there may be situations where private activity should be permitted because it genuinely does not harm anyone else – it simply suggests that we need to be extremely careful when we try to draw the boundary between private acts and their public implications.

Recreational drugs

If you can smoke and drink excessively in the privacy of your own home, why should you not be free to use other drugs, too? After all, you would be potentially harming no one but yourself. The counter argument is that harm is done through the illegal trade that makes those drugs available.

But those who argue for the legalisation of all recreational drugs can then make the point that it is their illegal status that encourages the crime and exploitation involved in a black market. Hence the harm is done by the illegality, not by the drugs themselves.

But even if there were no illegal trade, should you be allowed to harm yourself? Should medical care be provided for those who deliberately contribute to their illnesses? Accounts of drug abuse frequently speak of the impact on friends and family, so should the 'harm' principle extend to them?

The second objection is even more fundamental, from the perspective of political philosophy:

* It is that the state ought to be concerned with the moral welfare of citizens; they should not be left to decide what they will do to themselves.

We have already noted that Plato and Aristotle thought that the state had a responsibility to provide the conditions under which people could lead the good life – and therefore that questions determining the nature of such a good life were rightly part of political philosophy.

For Mill, however, the responsibility that the ancient Greeks gave to the state is now given to individuals. People are to determine *for themselves* what their good life will be, and the task of the state is to allow them to pursue that good life by all means possible, provided that it does not restrict the ability of all others to do the same.

But was he right to place so much emphasis on the individual? Today we recognize that people's views are coloured by the media and by the general attitudes of society, and these may both be influenced by governments. Governments are expected to take views on health, the environment, education, civil disobedience, respect for authority and so on. But by doing so they are influencing the sphere of life that Mill might have regarded as the responsibility of the individual alone. Therefore, given the nature of the media and society, is it fair to ask if Mill's individualistic approach is still a realistic one?

Basic freedoms

Of course, the degree of freedom to be allowed to the individual depends on whether you think that people, left to their own devices, will work together harmoniously, in which case you can allow them maximum freedom. If, like the philosopher Hobbes, you sense that, in their natural state, it is every man for himself with resulting chaos, then you will probably want to constrain freedom rather more.

Benjamin Constant (1768–1830), writing in France following the French Revolution and the rule of Napoleon, contrasted the 'Liberty of the Ancients', which was in effect the freedom to take part in republican political life, as exemplified in ancient Greece and Rome, with the 'Liberty of the Moderns', which he set out in terms of those things which individuals could do without fear of government control or restraint.

He sets out some basic freedoms, which are widely adopted as the minimum, namely, liberty of:

* religion
* opinion
* expression
* property.

He believed that society should protect each individual against punishment or constraint in striving for these four freedoms. Defining freedom in this way, of course, tends to promote an individualistic view of humankind – in other words, that we define ourselves mainly by what we as individuals choose to do, rather than seeing ourselves as small parts of a larger social whole.

Positive freedom

Positive freedom is the freedom to choose what we will do with our lives, to set goals and to work to achieve them. Should or can governments promote such freedom?

The danger with this approach, as presented by Berlin, is that there is a temptation to suggest that people should have a 'higher' freedom than that which they actually choose for themselves.

In other words, it is tempting for those in power to suggest that people are ignorant of their own potential and best interests.

There is a danger of telling people that they are truly free, when you have actually imposed upon them a notion of what they should be 'free' to do. And it is a short step from that to restraining people who have a lesser or more selfish notion of what they should be free to seek in life.

Berlin, in his lecture 'Two Concepts of Liberty', quotes Kant as saying 'Paternalism is the greatest despotism imaginable'. There is always the danger that a well-meaning reformer will come to treat people as material to be shaped by his chosen reforms, whether they choose to be so helped or not. And those imposed goals, and the imposed freedom to achieve them, are really just another form of control.

A clear example of the imposition of positive freedom is seen in the work of Rousseau. As we saw above, Rousseau argues that people's true happiness and freedom lies in setting aside their own particular wills and finding their true freedom by aligning themselves with the general will of the people. Rather than remaining slaves to their own passions and inclinations, they would then experience the freedom of giving themselves to the greater political enterprise. And, of course, if people do not recognize that their own best interest and freedom lay in that direction, they would have to be – in Rousseau's own chilling phrase – 'forced to be free'.

Mill opposed this approach. He said

Mankind are greater gainers by suffering each other to live as seems good to themselves, than by compelling each to live as seems good to the rest.

(On Liberty, p. 18)

Berlin argues that, for a society to be free, it is essential that no rules are regarded as absolute. In other words, it is always the right of the individual to interpret and understand a rule as it applies to him or her, and nobody should be forced to act in an inhumane way. It is also important for such freedom to be based on a definition of what it is to be a human being. People need to be able to develop an idea of the end or purpose of human life; they should be free to consider and discuss this, and to modify it as seems appropriate. In the end, this is not something that can be imposed on people, it is something that they have to embrace for themselves.

I complain that I cannot do what I want, therefore I am not free. You tell me that if I align my wants and goals with something else (namely what you think I should want) then I will be free to achieve them. But is freedom to conform true freedom?

Effective freedom

It is important to distinguish between being legally allowed to do something, and actually being able to go and do it. A law could be passed allowing everyone, if they so wish, to run a mile in two minutes. That would not, however, increase their *effective* freedom, because, although allowed to do so, they are physically incapable of it. Having a minimum of restrictions and a maximum of possibilities is fine, but in the real world most people will never have the opportunity either to become all that they are allowed to become, or to need to be restrained from doing everything that is possible for them to do. Their effective freedom depends on actually having the means and ability to do what they choose.

This idea of effective freedom relates back to the consideration of fairness. The quest for a fair society – whether through the sort of agreements suggested by Rawls, or through a utilitarian assessment of benefits – is at the same time a quest for a society in which *effective* freedom is maximized. To be treated unfairly is to have one's potential limited, and therefore to be denied things that would be possible if one had a fairer share of resources. Poverty is not just a matter of having insufficient money or resources, it is also about not being free to do the things that people with more money are freely able to choose to do.

It seems to me that a political system should be judged by the degree to which its people are able to take advantage of freedoms that are offered, not just by their entitlement to them.

The fundamental question: What difference does that freedom make to me?

Fear of freedom

The French existentialist philosopher Jean-Paul Sartre argued that existence precedes essence – in other words, we do not have a fixed self to which we need to conform, but we construct who we are as we go through life.

But this brings with it a terrible responsibility, namely that we are free to choose not just what we shall do, but also who we shall become. For Sartre and other existential philosophers, such as Martin Heidegger, this kind of freedom is something from which many people are tempted to run. It is a threat as well as a challenge. It is far easier to adopt some fixed role or mask than to be faced with the freedom to shape our own lives.

Freedom and the law

Both Rousseau and Kant argue that if laws were devised that were entirely rational, they would give freedom, because they would require people to do exactly what a rational person would want to do for him or herself anyway. This assumes that society is comprised of free individuals, each of whom is autonomous and acts in a rational way, both for his or her own benefit and in order to allow all others to do the same.

The problem – and it is a problem that we shall see repeated many times in the study of political philosophy – is that people do not live up to the standards set for them by some philosophers. If everyone were fully rational and not motivated by irrational impulses or their physical or emotional needs, then society would work perfectly on rational lines, and nobody would sense that their freedom was being constrained. However, life is not like that; we have a problem simply because people act from irrational motives, whether internal to themselves or externally imposed.

Hence, in practice, the law generally acts in line with the 'negative' rather than the 'positive' approach to freedom – in other words, it sets boundaries to the scope of freedom given to an individual. Law becomes a necessary protection to guard against the failure of reason and morality.

Mill saw law as a restriction of liberty. In all situations where you can get along without the law, it is fine to do so. If you cannot do so, then the law needs to be imposed to a degree sufficient to prevent one person's liberty from causing harm to others. Hence, a liberal society is likely to want a minimum of law, and thus a minimal government.

In whose interest?

Legislation would seem to be necessary when reason fails to deliver an acceptable result. But in whose interest should law be framed? If there is a dispute, each side may appeal to a legislator to offer a settlement or compromise. But is it ever possible to be sufficiently detached to be able to frame laws that are – and are seen to be – absolutely fair?

How do you decide between conflicting interests, where the freedom of one appears to preclude the freedom of the other?

Whether it is ever realistic to think that the law, or the government, can determine what I would freely want for myself if I were thinking rationally and objectively, may depend on a fundamental problem for philosophy. *Is society basically just a collection of individuals, or are individuals created by the society within which they live?*

The first possibility may seem obvious, and can lead to arguments about whether there is any such thing as society, over and above people and their families. The second possibility becomes reasonable once we recognize that almost everything we do, or think, or desire, comes as a result of communication or sharing in society. I could never aspire to be a doctor if I lived in a social vacuum – for being a doctor is about dealing with other people who are sick, the whole social notion of medicine, the way that it is funded and so on. So what appears to be an individual choice is in fact a socially conditioned option.

Freedom is always freedom *within* a society, it is a freedom to develop in ways that society may have suggested to me (positive freedom) and in ways that it allows (negative freedom) – but either way, it is a social phenomenon. *Solitary freedom is like the Zen notion of one hand clapping!*

6

rights, justice and the law

In this chapter we shall look at the basic rights that everyone should have in a just society, and then consider the problems that arise when the interests of the individual conflict with that of the majority of people. How far can you claim a right, if it goes against the general interest?

We see that, following Locke, justice, law and the rights of individuals are established with the consent of the people, rather than being imposed on them, and that this is fundamental to the whole process of representative democracy. We also note that natural rights are not those found in nature, but spring from a rational consideration of what human nature requires. And, of course, the whole idea of justice, rights and law depend on the establishment of proper political authority.

Among the many issues connected with gender and culture, for which there is no space in this present book, we shall briefly examine issues connected with political freedom and rights as they affect women.

We hold these truths to be self-evident, that all men are created equal, that they are endowed by their Creator with certain unalienable Rights, that among these are Life, Liberty and the pursuit of Happiness.

The American Declaration of Independence (1776)

The view that individuals have rights that should be upheld by law is a central feature of the broadly liberal approach to politics and is based on the two ideas we have already considered: equality and fairness.

But however 'self-evident' some truths may seem to be, they raise questions:

* How do you establish a fair balance between the rights of the individual and the political requirements of the state?
* How do you define justice? Do you start with the needs and aspirations of the individual and then assess how a state should enable them to be satisfied? Or do you start with the need to maintain a secure and prosperous state, and then assess what part individuals should be allowed or encouraged to play within it?
* Since control is exercised by law (or by brute force, if law breaks down) how do you ensure the independence of the judiciary, so that the law is not simply a tool of control in the hands of political leaders?

There is a whole range of issues here, but in this chapter we can touch on only some of them.

Justice handed down?

In *The Republic*, Plato argued that justice would benefit everyone in society; it was not simply a way of protecting the weak from the strong by offering them rights. Promoting justice was the result of seeing 'the good' itself, rather than being swayed by the passing interplay of events – the shadows on the back wall of the prisoners' cave.

But Plato thought that justice could not be understood by everyone, but only by those who were suitably educated.

The responsibility of the Guardians was therefore to grasp and hand down justice to the unenlightened. Individuals could flourish only if the state were well ordered, and if a 'noble lie' about the status of the lower orders was needed in order to keep them in their place, such bending of the truth was a price worth paying.

In other words, for Plato, justice and law were handed down to people from the Guardians, who alone knew what was in the people's own best interest and that of the *polis*.

Aristotle, equally, saw justice as the result of education in the virtues of tolerance and respect, but he also considered that the truest form of justice was a kind of friendship – in other words, a mutual exchange that could promote human flourishing. But he was realistic about who, in the *polis*, could establish such justice. In *Politics*, Book IV, he suggests that the state should be ruled by the middle classes, since the well-born tended to be arrogant and the poor to commit petty crimes, while the middle classes were more susceptible to rational argument!

Those with nothing to lose may take risks; those with most to lose are likely to be conservative and cautious. Does that suggest that those in the middle will be balanced and rational? I am far from sure that human nature works in quite that way.

So when it comes to rights, justice and the law, the Greeks were concerned primarily with the state rather than with the individual. You simply could not trust the majority of people to set their own laws. Citizens could take part in debates and vote, of course, but that process was not open to everyone, and although both would have accepted that a bad ruler might need to be overthrown, neither Plato nor Aristotle would have sanctioned lightly any form of public revolt.

Justice from the people

Article 21 of the United Nations Declaration of Human Rights states that: 'The will of the people shall be the basis of the authority of government'. In other words, it endorses democracy as the system of government best able to deliver human rights. And this follows from the whole social contract approach, which we examined in Chapter 3. Governments are set up through the agreement of the people, and part of that agreement is that individuals accept that they will be bound by the law that the government makes.

Governments establish political authority and impose that authority through law – that is a key feature of the internal stability and security of a state. The fundamental question to ask of a democratic system therefore is this: *To what extent is the law therefore produced by the people, as opposed to being imposed upon them?*

We shall return to this question later, in considering the place of legislation. For now, we need to keep in mind the fundamental issue of principle here – that within a democracy, it is the people who, through their elected representatives, shape what laws are passed. In addition, of course, we have the principle that the application of justice through the courts is separate from the executive power of government. This is designed to give added protection from the arbitrary use of government power.

Notice that, from a liberal–democratic point of view, justice is agreed between people, and may be applied on a utilitarian basis – laws are aimed at expressing the wishes of the majority of the people. This leaves out of account any question of what constitutes the good life, or human flourishing, and whether law can contribute to this. In a democracy, the government is not expected to improve the people, but to do what they want.

Rights

* What are the basic rights that every individual should be entitled to?
* How can those rights best be protected?
* Under what circumstances, and for what reason, should a state remove the rights of individuals? (For example, someone who has committed a crime, or is a danger to the public, might have the right of personal liberty removed, by being put in prison.)

In August 1789, the National Assembly of France, 'believing that the ignorance, neglect, or contempt of the rights of man are the sole cause of public calamities and of the corruption of governments', set out its *Declaration of the Rights of Man*, the first article of which declared that 'Men are born and remain free and equal in rights' and those 'natural' rights were said to be: freedom, property, security, and the right to resist oppression.

The rights that are set out in that declaration remain familiar: people are to be considered innocent until proven guilty; authority resides with the whole state, and not with factions; people have the right to security, property and freedom of speech. The general sense of the declaration is that the individual is to be free from the arbitrary exercise of power and protected by the law.

There are no rights in nature. The wildebeest, chased by lions, escapes into the river only to be devoured by crocodiles. There is no court to which the poor creature can appeal against being eaten. Life and death are determined by physical nature, strength and cunning. The strongest survive and breed, and thus each species develops.

The whole idea that people have rights which they can use to argue against some injustice done to them is the product of the system of agreements and laws that are established within the state. Rights and the law, and indeed the whole idea of justice, act as a check and balance to ensure protection for individuals. Rights would be redundant in a society where everything was done fairly to the satisfaction of all.

Hence 'natural rights' and 'natural law' are not found in nature, but are the result of nature being interpreted by human reason. So, for example, the most basic feature of a 'natural law' approach to ethics is that everyone has the right to self-defence – because clearly, defending your life is a basic function of all living things, and it would be unnatural to expect someone not to act to preserve themselves. But that is a rational interpretation – to say that everyone, when threatened, actually defends him or herself, is no more than an observation (and, of course, it may not always be true), but to say that everyone has a *right* to do so is quite a different thing – it is offering a reasoned justification for what happens.

Political authority

In *Leviathan* (1651), Hobbes clearly saw the danger of a lawless state where everyone was out for him or herself. Without security, there would be little scope for commerce or co-operative activity, and life would slide into a state of chaos and end up 'solitary, poor, nasty, brutish and short'. He therefore wanted people to accept the authority of a ruler, and to commit to accept that authority even if they themselves had played no part in setting it up.

Hobbes believed that once a government is established in a single person or a single assembly, all have to accept the authority of that ruler. Without that, Hobbes felt, there could be no guarantee of security. All have to give up their individual will on the condition that all others give up theirs as well, and thus all are equal in trusting the government that has been established.

However, Hobbes had a single 'get out' clause, and that was that one could refuse to accept the authority of a ruler in any case where one's life was threatened – a crucial and fundamental 'right'.

By contrast, Locke established the principle that government should be held to account by the people. Locke sees people as using the government as an *agent* of their own authority. Governments do what we want; if not, we replace them. The American Declaration of Independence made it clear (following principles set down by Locke) that a government derives its just powers from the consent of the governed, and that people have a right to dismiss that government and set up another. And, of course, that was the point of the Declaration, since the former colonies were complaining about and therefore breaking away from British rule.

And, of course, it was Locke's 'agency' approach to government that became the norm for justifying democracies.

For Locke, every individual is required to accept the majority decision, since this is the only way to get unified action, and because the government is given authority by people to act on their behalf. In the same way, people, through their social contract, agree that the government has a right to impose taxes and so on. But again, there is a limit to this. Locke holds that one should not be obliged to accept any situation where there is a direct threat to one's life or property – the same reservation made by Hobbes.

But here there is a fundamental problem. *How can society be stable if individuals have the right to reject their chosen rulers every time their own particular position is threatened by an action taken on behalf of a majority?*

It is, of course, exactly this problem of dealing with minorities that is a weakness of the utilitarian approach to political life. There needs to be some agreement on fairness or on basic rights that does not depend on a utilitarian assessment of the greatest benefit to the greatest number – otherwise, minorities lose out every time.

But at what point should you rebel against a government or a particular law? For Hobbes, it is the point at which your life is threatened. For Locke that same threat extends to your property. But that might be used to justify rebellion on the grounds of punitive taxation. Is that reasonable?

The logical alternative to the acceptance of political authority is anarchy – the view that each individual should be autonomous and self-governing, and that it is wrong and unnecessary to set up an external authority to control individuals in society. In other words, anarchy is the view that people should be left to organize their lives in their own way.

Anarchy is not just another term for chaos, it is a serious view and worthy of discussion. Almost everyone approves of some measure of anarchy, particularly in matters of sex. If you argue that what consenting adults do in private should remain outside the sphere of legislation, you are – to use the term correctly – in favour of 'anarchy' in the bedroom!

Legislation

What is the nature of law? How far can the law accurately put into effect the wishes of a ruler or government? The philosophy of law is a whole subject in itself, as is jurisprudence, and so we cannot start to examine exactly how the law operates. What we do need to do, however, is see how the operation of the law fits into the general requirement that a political system should promote justice, fairness, equality and freedom.

Although in *Statesman* Plato approves of the process of making and implementing laws, he sees them as *blunt instruments* compared with the sensitivity of a skilled philosophical ruler. This is because laws are inherently unable to see the subtleties and differences that distinguish one situation from another.

In other words, *law is a matter of compromise*. It cannot express, in each and every case, what a wise person would want to see as the outcome.

The crucial issue, if the law is going to be seen as just, is the sensitivity and flexibility with which it is applied. But even in case law, where the record of judicial decisions helps to guide the application of the law, it is never possible to take *all* the particularities of the present situation into account.

The French *Declaration of the Rights of Man* of 1789 described law as 'the expression of the general will' (a term that is found in Rousseau) and goes on to say that every citizen has a right, through his representative, to have a say in its foundation.

But it is important that the judiciary should be properly established and independent of external pressure. In the American Declaration of Independence, the complaint against the King was that 'He has obstructed the Administration of Justice by refusing his Assent to Laws for establishing Judiciary Powers' and 'He has made Judges dependent on his Will alone for the tenure of their offices, and the amount and payment of their salaries'.

Hence, the importance of separating out the three different functions of the state:

* The legislative body or parliament, which frames the laws and establishes the principles upon which the country is to be run.
* The executive, which puts those principles into action, taking as its authority the decisions of the legislature.

* The judiciary, which puts into practice the laws that have been put forward and agreed by the government.

The important principle is that, if the law is to be applied fairly, it must be independent of the power of the executive, and must not be influenced by any other authority or money.

In terms of rights and justice, the main thing to recognize here is that the law is an expression of the authority of the government. To ask whether it is ever right to protest against or break a law, is therefore equivalent to asking when it might be right to protest against or seek to change a government. Locke held that the government was accountable to the people. Logically, the law, too, must be so accountable. A law that does not have the broad consent of the people may be enforced, but without consent it is difficult to see how it could be described as just.

The proof of the pudding ...

David Hume was a philosopher who can generally be relied upon for sharp observation and common sense. He argues (in 'Of Civil Liberty', one of his *Essays Moral and Political*, 1741) that monarchies had improved recently, since they were:

> *found susceptible of order, method, and constancy, to a surprising degree. Property is there secure, industry encouraged, the arts flourish, and the prince lives secure among his subjects, like a father among his children.*

This is his straightforward way of judging the effectiveness of a political regime – that it leads to security and human flourishing. That seems to be a fair way to assess whether or not rights, justice and the law are well applied.

That remains true in the twenty-first century. To say that a country is democratic simply means that its leaders are elected; it does not imply that its people are free or that life is stable and civilized. Both Afghanistan and Iraq, for example, have elected governments, but that does not stop chaos and bloodshed. President Mugabe is an elected head of state in Zimbabwe, but that does not guarantee fairness or equality for its people. The key to a stable and civilized life for any nation is the application of a benign rule of law; 'benign' because the imposition of draconian legal restrictions by a military junta, for example, does little to secure the long-term co-operation of its people. Where the law is perceived to be fair, it is most likely to be obeyed. That in turn leads to respect for government and political stability.

Women and freedom

Mary Wollstonecraft (1759–97), whose *A Vindication of the Rights of Women*, 1792, was published the same year as Thomas Paine's *Rights of Man*, argues that men and women were equal on the basis of intellect, and is angry that men had assumed that they should be controlled by propriety, and restricted by prejudices. She is concerned particularly with education, believing that to be a major factor in preventing women from fulfilling themselves in society and working alongside men as equals. She boldly attacks and undermines the view of women presented by Rousseau:

> *Women are ... made slaves to their persons, and must render them alluring that man may lend them his reason to guide their tottering steps aright. Or should they be ambitious, they must govern their tyrants by sinister tricks, for without rights there cannot be any incumbent duties.*

(From *A Vindication of the Rights of Women*)

In other words she acknowledges and mocks what Rousseau saw as natural. She argues that a woman's first duty is to herself as a rational creature and as a mother. She makes the point that women are held back even from developing their own personal qualities, asking 'how can a being be generous who has nothing of its own? or virtuous, who is not free?' Wollstonecraft herself found intellectual stimulus by being a member of a group of thinkers which included Thomas Paine and, later, William Wordsworth. Her book should be seen against the background of radical political debate triggered by the revolution in France – ensuring that the rights of women, and their particular needs, were not neglected in the broader campaign for political rights.

Probably the best-known work to argue for women's equality, before the twentieth century, was John Stuart Mill's *The Subjection of Women*, 1869. Mill was of the opinion:

> *... that the principle which regulates the existing social relations between the two sexes – the legal subordination of one sex to the other – is wrong in itself, and now one of the chief hindrances to human improvement; and that it ought to be replaced by a principle of perfect equality, admitting no power or privilege to the one side, nor disability to the other.*

His campaign had an ideal precedent – the recent abolition of slavery in the USA. He says that, before its abolition, many people had argued that black people could not govern themselves, and therefore that slavery was entirely natural for them. The same argument had been used against women, and he now set out to refute it, and to argue that men and women should be treated equally.

He did not argue that women should be given any special treatment, simply that prejudices should be removed, and the law of supply and demand should determine their work and contribution.

Moving forward to the mid-twentieth century, another major work about the place of women in society is *The Second Sex*, 1949, by Simone de Beauvoir (1908–96). Her book explores the various myths about women and the roles they are expected to perform for the benefit of men – that of wife, lover, mother. In particular, she argues that women are not born to the roles that they end up adopting, but they accept them because that is what society expects.

She sums this up in her famous line 'One is not born, but rather becomes a woman'. Clearly, there is nothing natural about the position of women in society; it is (rather literally) man-made.

Society is as it is because that is what we choose it to be; it could be quite different. There is nothing inevitable about the place of women; they are not born to particular roles. There is nothing in the essence of womankind that holds her back from exploring her positive freedom.

Women and representation

Today, we take it for granted that a key feature of a successful democracy is adequate representation. In other words, if the political process is to reflect the wishes of the people, then the interests of all should be taken into account, both in terms of access to those who are elected to represent them, and in the selection of representatives in the first place.

It is worth pausing, therefore, to remember that women only received the right to vote in Britain in 1918, and even then it was restricted to women over the age of 30, who 'occupied premises of a yearly value of not less than £5'. It was not until 1928 that the voting age for women was brought into line with that of men.

The question now is not whether women have the right to vote, but whether the present system of elections provides sufficient representation for them within Parliament and government. Is the fact that there are more men than women in the British House of Commons simply a feature of social assumptions and opportunities which favour men?

Positive discrimination

In an ideal representative democracy, every group would be fairly represented in the decision-making process. The result would be that the general views of society and law would reflect the interests of all alike.

However, that is not always the case, and there are situations, for example, in employment law or the selection of candidates for election, where particular social groups feel that they are unjustly excluded or face particular obstacles in achieving parity with others.

In such cases, it may be argued that the balance should be restored by introducing positive discrimination. In other words, if all other things are equal, a decision should be made in favour of a representative of a group that feels it is unfairly treated. This can apply to women applying for work, for example, or members of a racial or religious group.

However, there may be problems with positive discrimination:

* The person appointed may not be accepted by his or her peers as having gained the position on the basis of his or her merits.
* There may be resentment on behalf of those who believe that they are better qualified but are now being discriminated against in favour of those who receive positive discrimination!

In an ideal situation, no discrimination of any sort would be practised, and therefore no positive discrimination would be needed. In such a situation, Mill's market-forces argument might work – that people would only do what they are best qualified to do. But even if that were put into practice fairly, it might still result in women not receiving the same treatment as men. Issues today include equal pay, or the 'glass ceiling' beyond which women do not seem to go in terms of promotion within a company.

The dilemma is whether market forces or positive discrimination are the best, long-term answer to remaining grievances. Those feminists who take a Marxist analysis argue that capitalism is inherently unfair on women and that men and women can only be treated equally when other social distinctions are also set aside. Today, with the dominance of capitalism and liberal democracy globally, the free-market approach (with minor social adjustments to promote equality) seems to be the most favoured.

7

nations, war and terrorism

So far in this book we have been able to do no more than touch on some of the central questions of Political Philosophy, but its modern agenda includes international relations, the sovereignty of states and global issues such as climate change and the political dimension of global markets.

In this final chapter, we can just touch on three of these issues. The first is the question of what, and how much, the state should do, and how much it should leave up to the individual. The second is the question of whether it is ever right to go to war against another nation and, if so, on what grounds it can be justified. The third, which in terms of the philosophical arguments is very much an extension of the second, is the question of how nation states should attempt to deal with the phenomenon of terrorism that is fuelled by religious or political ideology.

At the time of writing, there are 193 universally recognised sovereign states, of which 192 are members of the UN. (The exception is Vatican City, which is independent. Ten other states claim to be sovereign, but are not universally recognised as such.) States range in size from the huge Russian Federation to the compact Vatican City, but they have one thing in common – that they are recognized as autonomous political entities, each with its own government and legal system, and internationally accepted boundaries. Within their boundaries, they are 'sovereign' – in other words, they are self-governing, and may rightly object if other states try to interfere, or to invade their physical borders.

But autonomous nation-states, as we know them today, have emerged only during the last 300 years or so. When you go back to the time of the ancient Greeks, the political unit under discussion was the *polis*, or city-state; then there were kingdoms, empires, local self-governing republics, and areas where there was no single political structure at all. Until the eighteenth century, most of the world outside Europe was controlled by merchant companies, whose trading areas became colonies of whichever European power sponsored them. Australia was a wide open space waiting to be colonized, into which Britain sent convicts. Africa and South America were carved up by European powers – bringing some form of political control into areas being explored for commercial gain. The American colonies were ruled by Britain until 1783.

And even with the emerging of nationalism in the nineteenth century, there was still great flexibility in the shape of states. Both Germany and Italy were formed out of federations of smaller states. In the Middle East, the former Ottoman Empire was divided up into protectorates and newly formed states (with the later addition of Israel) whose boundaries were negotiated or imposed and therefore inherently unstable. Until the latter part of the twentieth century, even in Europe, there were changes in the borders and names of states – as happened particularly in the Balkans, with the break-up of the former Yugoslavia. The failure of Soviet communism in the 1980s profoundly affected the status of the previously satellite soviet states, as they gained independence.

Warfare has always been a feature of competition between kingdoms and empires within Europe, but the rise of nationalism only encouraged inter-state rivalry, and competitive pressure for dominance within Europe contributed to two world wars.

The League of Nations, set up in 1920 after the trauma of World War I, attempted to stabilize Europe, but failed because of the expansionist actions of Germany and Italy – in other words, it lacked the power to authorize compliance with its desired aims. The UN was set up in 1945. One of the key issues for political philosophy is the extent to which it (or any other) international body can have authority over individual states.

Not our subject!

All this is a matter of political geography, rather than political philosophy, but some study of the way in which nations have changed provides a useful corrective to the over-abstract analysis of some philosophical texts. Thus there is little point in using the term 'state' without some idea of the range of states today and how they are run. So dipping into political geography gives a valuable backdrop to philosophical arguments.

Nations and states

So far we have used the terms 'nation' and 'state' rather loosely. They now need to be clarified, and for our purposes they may be simply defined as:

* Nation – a physical area, whose inhabitants have a sense of shared history, common territory, language and culture. A nation can become a state, or a state can give rise to a nation.
* State – a sovereign political authority. It may or may not correspond to a nation.

Nations are visible. A nation comprises a geographical area, with its people, language, traditions and so on, in so far as they form an identifiable entity. Nations have a long history and may have gone through many political upheavals.

By contrast, states are relatively invisible. A state is a political entity, comprising – in the case of a democracy – a parliament for deciding upon national strategies and laws, an executive for carrying out the business of government, and a judiciary for putting into effect the laws that a parliament has approved. It also comprises those bodies that control security – the police, in terms of internal security, and the armed forces for external security.

The state is therefore a set of political structures and power relations, agreed (or imposed) on the people of a nation, in order to provide the benefits of government and law. States can be changed – both in terms of their status and their boundaries – *because they are artificial constructions, not chunks of land.*

What should the state do?

Government, even in its best state, is but a necessary evil; in its worst state, an intolerable one.

Thomas Paine, *Common Sense*, 1776

Aristotle's aspiration was that the state could and should encourage people to live well. At the other extreme, Paine saw it as a 'necessary evil' – a view taken up by political anarchists. Part of the task of political philosophy is to try to arrive at a view of exactly how much government can and should do. Some see it as crucial in protecting human rights and controlling the negative aspects of human behaviour. Others see society as well able to take care of itself, and wish government simply to provide the minimum political structure within which freedom can operate.

But the fundamental issue raised here is really about the *amount* that the state should do – since the more it gathers in tax the more it is able to do by way of social provision and so on.

Thomas Hobbes argued that the sovereign had four duties:
* to defend the nation against foreign enemies
* to preserve peace and internal security
* to allow subjects to enrich themselves
* to allow 'harmless liberty' (i.e. freedom that does not threaten security).

The assumption here is that people do not want to be involved politically. What they really care about is their economic welfare, and once they are secure from threats both external and internal, what they want is the freedom to increase their wealth. Provided their actions do not endanger security, they are free to do them. This is the starting point for what might be described as a 'minimalist' view of the work of the state.

In 'On Anarchy', a section from the second part of his *Rights of Man*, Thomas Paine says:

> **The more perfect civilization is, the less occasion has it for government, because the more does it regulate its own affairs, and govern itself.**

This approach, which is broadly *liberal*, is concerned to allow individuals maximum control of their own lives. Health and education should be the responsibility of individuals, banding together to organize health insurance and to pay for schools. By way of concession, a minimum is provided to ensure that the poorest receive some help, but as an ideal, the poor should be encouraged to work to improve their situation and no longer have to rely on state aid.

This is the opposite of the broadly *socialist* approach, where the state takes responsibility for the welfare of its citizens, and taxes everyone to a level sufficient to cover the costs. The argument here is that provision of planned services is fairer and more effective than leaving everything to the open market, with the minimum of safety nets. On the other hand, the problem with such a view is that – as with the totally planned economy of the communist state – universal provision too often leads to inefficiency, bureaucracy and lack of accountability.

Changing governments

There is a fundamental question that hangs over all political structures. What if they go wrong? What if they fail to meet the aspirations of the people over whom they rule? What if they repress minorities? What if they are seen to be corrupt or self-serving?

Leabharlann
Chontae Ceatharlach

In a democracy, voters are able to express their dissatisfaction at the polls, although that, of course, is not guaranteed to bring about the required change. Unless there is an overall majority for one particular party in a majority of constituencies, there will be a process of negotiation before a government can be appointed that commands a majority of the elected representatives.

But what if that democratic process is not available? What if a government forbids democratic elections for whatever reason? At what point would it then be right to use direct action – or, if necessary, violence – to bring about a change?

One way of evaluating this would be by a utilitarian assessment. How do you assess the benefits to be gained by regime change, against the potential loss of life that might come from the attempt at revolution? And how do you estimate that cost against the cost of the continuation of the current government? Thus, for example, one of the debates following the 2003 Iraq war, once the issue of weapons of mass destruction was no longer viable as justification, was the harm done to the Iraqi people by allowing Saddam Hussein to continue in power. The problem with the present violence in that country is that, on a utilitarian assessment, it is less obvious that overall people are better off than they were before. *That matter is debatable, but the principle on which the judgement was made is utilitarian.*

The other option is to say that, even if the overthrow of the government might cause more suffering than it prevents, it is still worthwhile to change a government that does not respect certain human rights. In other words, as a matter of principle, certain governments should be opposed, no matter what the cost.

The extreme version of that argument is that of the terrorist who claims that the loss of innocent human life is a necessary and worthwhile price to pay for the possibility of regime change. But that view is generally only taken by those whose views are absolute and fundamental – in other words, it is not the result of some balancing of possibilities, but a campaign in which self-sacrifice is made worthwhile in the greater scheme of things.

The just war theory

It can be argued that warfare and other violent confrontations are not an inevitable feature of international politics, but happen because there is no effective alternative. Here is the view of Hannah Arendt:

> *The chief reason warfare is still with us is neither a secret death wish of the human species, nor an irrepressible instinct to aggression, nor, finally and more plausibly, the serious economic and social changes inherent in disarmament, but the simple fact that no substitute for this final arbiter in international affairs has yet appeared on the political scene. Was not Hobbes right when he said: 'Covenants, without the sword, are but words'?*

On Violence, Hannah Arendt (1969)

So the first and crucial thing to acknowledge is that war represents failure to secure a rational way of resolving disputes, and can only be justified (if at all) if all possible avenues for peaceful resolution have been explored and are found blocked.

There are two questions to be considered:
* When is it right to go to war? (*jus ad bellum*)
* What rules should apply to the conduct of a war?
  (*jus in bello*)

The principles of the just war, set out by Thomas Aquinas in the thirteenth century and subsequently developed, are broadly that it may be just to go to war if:
* it is conducted by proper authority (this is generally taken to imply that war should be carried out by a state, not by an individual or group)
* there is a valid reason to go to war (for example, in self-defence if threatened by another state)
* warfare is a proportional response to whatever has happened, and there is a reasonable chance of success. (In other words, massive retaliation as a result of a minor border infringement would be ruled out, as would launching a war when it was clear that little could be achieved by the resulting slaughter.)

* the intention of going to war is to establish peace and justice. (War is not valid as an end in itself.)

The conduct of war is considered right only if:

* it is waged against military personnel, not against civilians (in other words the loss of civilian life should minimized)
* the force used is proportional (so, for example, a minor border dispute should not be used as an excuse for an all-out military assault)
* minimum force is used in order to achieve the war's aim (this would preclude using weapons of mass destruction, or excessive carpet bombing, if less force could achieve the same military objectives)

The other responsibility, considered under the 'just war' heading, may be termed *jus post bellum*. This is the responsibility of a victor to ensure that the vanquished state is made stable and viable. In other words, it would be considered wrong to invade a state, destroy its military and political structures, and then withdraw to leave its people in chaos. Forced regime change implies a responsibility to establish a viable alternative.

In terms of political philosophy, the fundamental questions are:

* Is it possible to construct a world order in which the danger of war between states is reduced?
* Is it possible to do so without at the same time having an international military capability sufficient to ensure that all states comply?
* At what point are individual states likely to abandon their own military control in favour of an international body?

It is clear, for example in the debate leading up to the 2003 Iraq war, that individual states cannot be forced to comply with the wishes of the UN. But does that suggest that the UN itself, as a body, should be able to adjudicate between states and enforce its rules through military action?

In the end, there is a limit to what military force can do in the political arena. It can impose a settlement where there is a dispute, but it cannot guarantee the agreement of all parties to the dispute, nor persuade of the fairness of the result. As David Miliband, then British Foreign Secretary, said at the Labour Party conference in September 2007: 'While there are military victories there never is a military solution'.

And, of course, where people feel that they have been unfairly treated, whether as a result of military intervention or exploitation by a dominant trading partner, they may feel powerless to change the existing political or economic structures by legal democratic means, and be driven to take some form of direct action. A sense of injustice lies behind the phenomenon which, while not new, now commands global attention: terrorism.

Terrorism

The attack on New York and the Pentagon, Washington, on 11 September 2001 was, without doubt, instrumental in a major re-think of security ways in which states can counter the threat of terrorism. There were terrorist attacks before that, including extended campaigns like that of the IRA in Northern Ireland and the Basque separatist movement (ETA) in Spain, but it was the sheer scale and location of 9/11 that made it so significant.

The literature is already extensive, and cannot realistically be reviewed here, but some recent books (for example, Francis Fukuyama's *America at the Crossroads*) have explored and attempted to evaluate the political significance of that event and the resulting 'war on terror'.

With the rise of the modern nation state, warfare and threats came to be seen as a state-against-state phenomenon. The scale of the power and weaponry held by states, as opposed to private individuals and groups, made it seem inconceivable that a serious threat could come other than from another state. That is no longer the case. The attacks on 11 September 2001 were carried out by an organization that is transnational. Just as a multinational company can have branches throughout the world, so it seems an organization that has political or violent ends can be global. This creates a very special problem, for states are equipped to fight other states; they are not equipped to fight networks of individuals or small groups.

That was the problem that faced the USA after the attack on New York. It would have been easy if one particular state could be shown to be responsible – a quick and decisive war might have eliminated the problem. It was not to be so easy, as the wars in Afghanistan and Iraq have shown.

The 'just war' theory is designed to apply to state-on-state violence, but it can equally be used to highlight the nature of terrorism: terrorists do not represent any accepted 'authority', nor do they generally, although there are exceptions, respect civilian loss of life, nor can their actions be deemed proportionate, since it is often unclear what the aim of the terrorist attack is, other than to do damage.

The only principle that might be used to justify terrorism would be the argument that, if one's life and property is threatened, one has the right to defend oneself – a principle set out by both Hobbes and Locke. Terrorism might then be seen as a form of *self-defence*, where the imbalance of weapons and power would make it impossible to secure a just outcome through direct military confrontation. But such an argument would also need to show that all peaceful means of achieving the terrorists' stated goals had been exhausted. The problem is that, since a terrorist group is not a nation-state, it is difficult for it to enter into bilateral talks in the first place, since governments frequently declare that they will not talk to or negotiate with terrorists.

The principles by which a war can be deemed just can also be applied to the military response to terrorism, but here there are considerable problems. A key question is: *Is a nation to be held responsible for a terrorist group that may operate from within its geographical boundaries?*

Afghanistan was very clearly a base for al-Qaeda operations, and it was on that basis that the USA went on the offensive in that country, deposing the Taliban regime that had supported the terrorists. But what of Pakistan, which opposes and takes military action against such terrorist groups, but acknowledges that they operate within its territory? What of Britain and other western-European countries? If a terrorist cell based in Britain had carried out at attack in another country, would that justify direct action by the forces of that country on British soil?

The basis upon which the USA launched the war on terror was that of pre-emptive action. Americans no longer considered that they should wait to be attacked and then retaliate; they were prepared to take the fight to the enemy. The idea of preventative war was born: where a threat, or potential threat, could be identified, it was deemed appropriate to take whatever action was necessary, including the use of force.

That principle, coupled with evidence (later shown to be incorrect) that Iraq had weapons of mass destruction that were capable of threatening international security, led to the Iraq war of 2003. It was argued that, if Iraq (or any other nation) were to provide weapons of mass destruction to a terrorist group, the results could be catastrophic.

There were two major problems with this:

* A state, going to war against another state, can occupy that state and replace its government. However, military action cannot subdue a religious or political ideology. If anything, as has been demonstrated in Iraq, an ideology is strengthened when it faces a visible enemy, since it feeds on all the resentment caused by the inevitable casualties of war.

* Because an international terrorist group is based ideologically and not geographically, it cannot be subdued through conventional military conquest. In other words, whatever national target is selected, it is bound to be wrong, and hitting a wrong target always helps the enemy.

There is, of course, another approach. Terrorism thrives on perceived injustice. People join terrorist organizations because they believe there is a cause to be fought for, an injustice deserving a terrorist response. If the causes of that injustice are removed, then there is less reason for people to resort to terror, and less reason for others to give them shelter or tacit support.

To parody Tony Blair on crime, a balanced moral and philosophical approach to terror might be: 'Tough on terror; tough on the causes of terror'.

There is an additional problem with any attempt to counter terrorism. Terrorists, by their very nature, do not abide by just war principles or established conventions (for example, the Geneva Convention on the treatment of prisoners). The temptation, therefore, is to counter terrorists by using methods that equally flout those principles and conventions (for example, illegal detention of suspects without trial; torture and inhumane treatment of prisoners; 'special rendition' of prisoners from one country to another for the purposes of torture or imprisonment).

However, a nation retains its credibility and its standing within the international community to the extent that it maintains the highest standards of integrity in both its domestic and foreign policy. The danger is that by attempting to fight terrorism on its own terms, a nation state is liable, not only to lose the battle on the ground, but also to lose its international standing. This point was made succinctly by Michael Ignatieff in his Gifford Lectures in Edinburgh in 2003. Recognizing that defeating terrorism requires violence, he asked: 'How can democracies resort to these means without destroying the values for which they stand?'